"It may be true that people should try harder to cultivate a taste for extra-nutritious foods, but unless they themselves desire to change their tastes, mealtimes can turn into lectures or worse. I recommend a more diplomatic approach—serving nutritious 'mickey finns.' "

Mrs. Sutton's delicious mouth-watering recipes make eating health foods a delight. Here, within easy reach, is all the wonderful goodness from traditional farm-home kitchens!

NANCY SUTTON lives with her two young sons on a tiny farm near New Hope, Pennsylvania. She is a member of the Cheltenham (Pa.) Chapter of the Natural Food Associates; she regularly airs her opinions about health foods and nutrition on a local radio station. Well known as a cook, she sells her home-baked bread, cookies and cakes to neighbors and fellow members of the food association.

ADVENTURES IN COOKING WITH HEALTH FOODS

Nancy Sutton

PYRAMID BOOKS ● NEW YORK

This book is dedicated to:
all those who love good food
and desire good health.

ADVENTURES IN COOKING WITH HEALTH FOODS

A PYRAMID BOOK
Published by arrangement with Frederick Fell, Inc.

Pyramid edition published September, 1971
    Second printing March, 1972

Library of Congress Catalog Card Number: 69-10770

Printed in the United States of America

Pyramid Books are published by Pyramid Communications, Inc. Its
trademarks, consisting of the word "Pyramid" and the portrayal of
a pyramid, are registered in the United States Patent Office. Pyramid
Communications, Inc., 919 Third Avenue, New York, N. Y. 10022.

CONTENTS

ooooooooooo

INTRODUCTION

~~~~~~~~~~~~~~~~~~~~~~~~~~~~

Although there are quite a few cookbooks which deal with the use of natural foods, I've found that many of the recipes are unpalatable to the average person. Many times I've had to chuck a whole recipe which in itself wasn't a cooking failure, because my family just wouldn't eat it. It may be true that people should try harder to cultivate a taste for extra-nutritious foods, but unless they themselves desire to change their tastes, mealtimes can turn into lectures or worse. Instead of lecturing, I recommend a more diplomatic approach—serving nutritious "mickey finns."

This book is written for women who thrive in the kitchen. Home baking is especially recommended. It will help you keep your food budget in line, for you can usually cut the costs in half over commercially baked goods and at the same time produce delicious bread, rolls, cakes, cookies, and pies with high nutritional quality, which often are not available at any price. Dollar for dollar the commercial baker will not produce what you can produce in your natural habitat.

Our present day commercial food production mechanisms are set to mass-produce packaged merchandise. When you begin with the pristine ingredients and pour your own labor into the batter, you can produce in your kitchen the ultimate value, dollar for dollar, ounce for ounce.

It has yet to be proved that the modern (preservative-additive) foods are superior to grandmother's foods. For this reason, the author uses grandmother's primitive ingredients, untampered with by modern man.

The following recipes are a synthesis of gourmet and nutritious cookery.

6

GLOSSARY OF SPECIAL INGREDIENTS

(usually available at health food stores
and sometimes available in supermarkets)

∞∞∞∞∞∞∞∞∞∞∞

Arrowroot—A flour used as a thickener, made from the roots of the tropical cassava plant. Arrowroot may be substituted for cornstarch, using approximately 4 T. of the arrowroot for 3 T. cornstarch.

Baking Powder—I use single-action Royal baking powder. If you use double-action baking powder, you will need to use less in my recipes. See your baking powder label. Special baking powders with a cereal-free base for people on special diets are available.

Carob—Pods from the Ceratonia Siliqua tree. These pods are ground up into a flour or powder (I prefer the finer powder type). Candy made from carob is available, and tastes like milk chocolate bars. Carob may be substituted for chocolate if one is allergic to chocolate. Carob does not contain the oxalic acid (which interferes somewhat with calcium absorption)* or the stimulant theobromine, both of which are present in chocolate and cocoa. Also, since carob

---

* Adelle Davis, *Let's Cook It Right*, (New York: Harcourt, Brace & World, 1947), pp. 445-6.

is naturally sweet, it does not require the large amount of sugar necessary to make chocolate sweet. Carob is sometimes called St. John's bread because it is thought by some that the locusts mentioned in the Bible as being a mainstay of John the Baptist's diet were really carob pods.

Coconut—Freshly grated coconut is extra delicious and it freezes beautifully. In order to shell a coconut, first open up 2 of the 3 eyes at the top with a screwdriver. Shake out the milk and save to drink. Place the coconut in a hot oven (about 400°F.). In about 15 to 20 minutes you should see a few cracks in the shell. At that time, remove it from the oven, place on a sturdy counter, and give it a good whack with a hammer; the shell should fall right off. You may have to pry it just a little with the tip of a knife in some spots. Wash and peel off the brown inner skin with a vegetable peeler. Grate and refrigerate or freeze as is. One medium coconut makes about 3 cups grated coconut.

Flours—Potato, rice, soy, rye, whole wheat, and unbleached white flours are used in recipes in this book. If you use white flour in any of your recipes, 1 T. of wheat germ may be added to each cup of flour to improve nutritional value. I keep my white flour already mixed with wheat germ in my canister. For the recipes in this book, however, I have listed the wheat germ as a separate ingredient.

Soy flour can often be substituted for up to one-fourth of the flour in baked goods to bring up the nutritional value. Soy flour is very high in protein— as high as 200 grams of protein per pound—whereas white flour usually runs around 50 grams per pound. Since soy flour browns readily, you may need to reduce your oven temperature about 25°F. if you are altering your own recipes by substituting soy flour for part of the regular flour.

Honey—Since honey contains some vitamins and minerals and white sugar contains none, I substitute honey for white sugar in recipes whenever possible. Honey is sweeter than sugar, so less is needed. There are many kinds of honey, depending on the source of the pollen the bees use to make the honey. One of the mildest flavored and most common honeys is clover honey.

Lecithin Granules—A rather bland-tasting granular extract from soy beans. It is rich in choline and inositol (two B complex vitamins involved in fat metabolism). It is used as a diet supplement and may be added to some recipes.*

Molasses—Blackstrap molasses is the last extraction from sugar cane and is very rich in B vitamins and iron. I prefer to mix blackstrap half and half with regular molasses so the resulting product is not so strong tasting. I prefer the molasses to be of the un-sulphured variety.

Monosodium Glutamate—A bland seasoning often used in Chinese cookery and in other dishes of vegetable origin. Trade name is Accent.

Nuts—I usually shell my own nuts. That way they are cheaper, fresher, and I'm sure no chemicals have been added, as they sometimes are to forestall rancidity. In regard to peanut butter, I feel the old-fash-

---

* Adelle Davis, *Let's Eat Right to Keep Fit*, (New York: Harcourt, Brace & World, 1954), p. 41.

ioned peanut butter with nothing but salt added tastes far superior to the hydrogenated variety.

Oil, Vegetable—Corn, cottonseed, peanut, safflower, or soy oil may be used for general cooking and baking. Olive oil is good for Italian food or for salad dressing if you like it. I prefer oil without any additives.

Pepper—Freshly ground black pepper tastes much better than the pre-ground kind. You need a pepper-mill in order to grind it as you need it.

Salt—I use vegetable salt for cooking. It has dried vegetables mixed with the iodized salt and gives a delicious flavor to food. The trade name is Vege-Sal. For baking, either sea salt or regular iodized salt may be used.

Sugar, Raw—A granular form of sugar, amber in color and not as refined as white sugar. It may be equally substituted for white sugar in recipes as it does not alter the recipe as brown sugar or honey might do.

Stock, Chicken or Beef—I prefer the chicken and beef flavor bases instead of the bouillon cubes, because the paste-like bases have a better flavor. They are often available in supermarkets and are sold in 4 oz. glass jars. The usual dilution of the stock is 1 T. of the base to 1 cup hot water.

Wheat Germ—The germ of the wheat from whence springs the new life when the grain of wheat is planted. It is extracted from the wheat and is concentrated in the B complex and E vitamins. It is rarely ever put back into baked goods commercially. Don't try to use raw wheat germ in your bread recipes, as the bread won't rise properly. I use the vacuum-packed toasted wheat germ sold in most supermarkets.

Yeast—I use granular yeast. If you use cake yeast, one cake equals one package, or 1 T., dry granular yeast. Cake yeast should be dissolved in 95°F. water and dry granular yeast in 105°F. water before adding to dough.

Yeast, Brewers or Primary—This is dried yeast which has lost its leavening power, but is extremely rich in the B complex vitamins. Many kinds are available, such as celery or bacon flavored varieties. Sometimes it is sold in supermarkets.

CHART FOR SUBSTITUTION OF OIL FOR SOLID SHORTENING

For 1 T. fat	substitute	1 T. oil
2 T. fat	"	1½ T. oil
4 T. fat	"	3 T. oil
⅓ cup fat	"	4 T. oil
½ cup fat	"	6 T. oil
¾ cup fat	"	⅔ cup plus 1 T. oil
1 cup fat	"	½ cup plus 2 T. oil
2 cups fat	"	1½ cups oil

Note—These substitutions are for baking, not cooking. Most recipes take kindly to the oil substitution, but certain cookies tend to become very crumbly with oil.

INSTRUCTIONS FOR SPROUTING WHEAT, MUNG BEANS, AND ALFALFA SEEDS

Soak 1 cup washed and cleaned whole wheat berries, mung beans or seeds for 24 hours in warm water to cover. Drain. Place in special clay sprouting dish with water in bottom compartment, seeds on next part of sprouter, and cover with lid. If you don't have a sprouting dish, you may use a colander lined with a clean, wet, white cotton cloth. Place seeds on cloth and fold cloth over to keep seeds damp. Place colander in a larger bowl filled with water so that water just barely touches colander. Place a plate over top. Next day rinse off the sprouts and change water in bottom. Wheat is ready to eat when sprouts are about ⅜ of an inch long. Don't let roots develop, or the taste will change. Wheat should be ready in one to two days of sprouting in dish or colander. Mung beans or alfalfa seeds may be permitted to grow longer than the wheat, but don't permit any leaves to form or the taste will be very greenish. These sprouts may be eaten as is, or used in various cooked dishes. The wheat may be eaten for breakfast with milk or yogurt or added to a bread recipe. (See Whole Wheat Raisin Bread Variation.) Mung beans may be added to Chinese food, to scrambled eggs to make Egg Foo Yong, or to salads or soups. Alfalfa seeds are good on salads.

When a seed is sprouted, it greatly increases in vitamin value and Vitamin C is generated by the sprouting seed. Seeds have been an important source of Vitamin C in the Chinese diet for many years.

APPETIZERS

∞∞∞∞∞∞∞∞∞∞∞∞

MACADAMIA NUT CHEESE FILLING
MAKES 1 CUP
(FOR CELERY OR SANDWICHES OF DATE NUT OR BOSTON BROWN BREAD)

Mix together ½ cup cream cheese or creamed cottage cheese, ¼ cup chopped macadamia nuts, and ¼ cup chopped dried apricots (unsulphured). Fill the celery or sandwiches.

Note—Some unsulphured dried apricots are quite dry and will require soaking in warm water for a few minutes. Turkish unsulphured apricots are soft because they are only partially dried. They also retain their natural orange color.

GARLIC CHEESE DIP
MAKES 1 CUP

½ cup creamed cottage cheese
½ cup mayonnaise (low calorie salad dressing may be substituted)
¼ t. salt (preferably vegetable salt)
¼ t. garlic powder
2 T. chopped fresh parsley
dash pepper
1 T. vinegar

Mix all ingredients together and serve as a dip for raw vegetables.

LIVERWURST DIP
MAKES ABOUT 1½ CUPS

8 oz. liverwurst (liver sausage may be substituted)
¾ cup sour cream or yogurt
½ t. dill seed
1 t. minced onion.

Combine in a bowl with a mixer. May be used as a dip, or to fill celery or sandwiches.

CREAM CHEESE AND DRIED BEEF FILLING
MAKES 1 CUP

one 4-oz. package dried beef
8 oz. cream cheese or Neufchatel cheese
1 T. prepared yellow mustard

Chop dried beef fine. Cream the cheese and mix with the beef and mustard. Use to fill celery or to make sandwiches.

HERRING MOUSSE
SERVES 6

¼ cup butter (preferably unsalted)
one 7-oz. can water-packed solid white-meat tuna fish, drained
¼ t. salt (preferably vegetable salt)
¼ cup pickled herring (preferably packed in wine), drained
pinch garlic powder

Melt the butter. Pour into a blender. Add the tuna and blend till paste-like. Add remaining ingredients and blend till smooth. Pack into small buttered bowl. Refrigerate for a few hours. Turn out onto a plate and surround with small pieces of good rye or pumpernickel bread.

BRAZIL NUT CHIPS
MAKES 1 CUP

1 lb. Brazil nuts (in shells)
2 T. melted butter or oil
¼ to ½ t. salt

To shell the nuts, cover them with water in a sauce-pan and bring to a boil. Simmer 5 minutes. Drain and shell. Cut into lengthwise slices about ⅛ inch thick. Spread on a baking tray, drizzle butter or oil over nuts, sprinkle with salt, stir around with a fork, and bake at 350°F. for 10 minutes, stirring frequently with a fork to keep from burning. Cool.

HOT CHINESE CHICKEN LIVER APPETIZERS
MAKES APPROXIMATELY 20

Marinade: Combine 3 T. soy sauce, ¼ cup water, ½ t. monosodium glutamate, ⅛ t. garlic powder and ¼ t. pepper
Appetizers: ½ lb. chicken livers, cut in half, one 5-oz. can Chinese water chestnuts, cut in half, ½ lb. sliced bacon, slices cut in half

Place a piece of liver and a slice of water chestnut on one end of bacon strip, roll tightly and insert a heavy toothpick through all. Place in a bowl, pour on marinade, cover, and refrigerate for several hours or longer. Remove from marinade and bake at 450°F. for 20 minutes, turning once. Serve immediately.

PEANUT SUNFLOWER SPREAD
(USE AS A SPREAD FOR BREAD OR CRACKERS, OR
TO FILL CELERY)

1 cup old-fashioned peanut butter (just peanuts and salt)
½ cup shelled raw sunflower seeds

Soften the peanut butter with a spoon and stir in
the sunflower seeds.

MIXED FRUIT COMPOTE
SERVES 8 TO 10

½ fresh pineapple
3 grapefruit
3 oranges
1 cup fresh, frozen, or canned peaches or apricots
3 bananas
2 ripe pears
one 10-oz. package frozen strawberries
(slightly thawed)
2 cups fresh strawberries may be substituted
1 cup seedless grapes (optional)
1 cup sweet fresh cherries (optional)
¼ cup Triple Sec liqueur (sweet wine may
be substituted)

Mix together pineapple and the sectioned grape-
fruits and oranges with their juice. Add the peaches
or apricots, sliced bananas, diced pears, slightly
thawed strawberries, grapes (cut in half if desired)
and cherries. Pour liqueur or wine over the fruit. This
may be served at once or refrigerated for a few minutes to let the flavors mellow. If it is going to be held
in the refrigerator for more than a few minutes, wait
till the last minute to add the diced pears and sliced
bananas so they don't get mushy or brown. Other

fruits, such as raspberries, blueberries, or melon balls, may be added. This fruit mixture may be served in scooped-out pineapple shells, cut lengthwise with foliage left on for a festive touch.

ROSY SPICED EGGS
MAKES 12

6 medium-sized beets (or a 1-pound can of beets)
2 cups cider vinegar
¼ cup honey
2 cloves garlic, sliced
1 T. mixed pickling spices
1 t. salt
12 hard-cooked eggs (shelled)

Boil the unpeeled beets with 1 inch of their stems on. When tender, drain, peel, and halve. Mix the beets with the remaining ingredients, except the eggs. Let set 30 minutes. Remove the beets from the liquid. Pour the liquid over the shelled eggs in a quart jar or bowl (not metal). Cover the eggs completely. Refrigerate for 24 hours. Drain. Serve as an appetizer, for a picnic lunch, or with a salad.

The recipe below calls for grated orange and lemon rinds. Since I prefer organically grown oranges which have not been artificially colored, I freeze the citrus rind for cooking whenever I am able to purchase the organic fruit. It is a great convenience to have the grated rind available in your freezer ready at a moment's notice, since it does not need to be thawed before use.

MINTY FRUIT APPETIZER
SERVES 4

SYRUP:
> 1 cup water
> ¼ cup honey
> 2 T. chopped fresh or frozen mint leaves
> 4 t. lemon juice
> 1 t. grated orange rind
> 1 t. grated lemon rind
> 1 T. additional fresh or frozen chopped mint leaves

FRUIT:
> ½ fresh diced pineapple (frozen may be substituted)
> 1 cup fresh or frozen blueberries
> 1 orange

Mix all ingredients for syrup together except the last tablespoon of mint leaves. Bring mixture to a boil in a small saucepan, reduce heat, cover, and simmer 15 minutes, uncovering during the last 5 minutes of the cooking time. Strain and cool. When cool, add the mint leaves. Cover and refrigerate several hours or overnight. Strain before using. If using frozen fruit, thaw fruit partially before serving. Cut the orange in half and section like a grapefruit. Squeeze out the orange juice over the orange sections and add it to the diced pineapple and blueberries. Pour mint syrup over all and refrigerate ½ to 1 hour before serving. Garnish with mint leaves if desired.

MELON BALLS
SERVES 6

2 cups each cantaloupe, honeydew, and
watermelon balls
¼ cup Triple Sec liqueur

Pour Triple Sec over the melon balls and let stand
in the refrigerator ½ hour or so for flavors to blend before serving.

Note—Triple Sec is an orange-flavored liqueur.
Sweet wine may be substituted.

SALADS

∞∞∞∞∞∞∞∞∞∞∞

NANCY'S TOSSED SALAD
WITH CROUTONS
SERVES 6

1 small head lettuce
2 to 3 stalks celery
2 medium carrots
½ of a cucumber
½ of a green pepper
⅓ cup chopped walnuts or pecans (optional)
6 slices bacon, fried, drained, and crumbled (optional)
2 sliced tomatoes if in season (or use 1 cup cherry tomatoes)
2 quartered hard-cooked eggs (optional)
croutons (recipe given below)

Wash lettuce well, dry, and tear into bite-sized pieces. Other greens may be used in place of part of the lettuce. You should have approximately 1 quart of greens. Prepare other vegetables and add to the lettuce in the salad bowl. Slice the celery on the diagonal into ½ inch slices. Cut the carrots into paper thin slices with a vegetable peeler, or grate coarsely. Cut the cucumber into ¼-inch slices. (If you are sure that the cucumber has not been waxed or sprayed, you may leave the skin on and score the skin lengthwise all the way around before cutting into slices—this will make the cucumber slices very attractive.) Refrigerate the salad until serving time. Fry the bacon till crisp, drain, and crumble. Chop the nuts, slice the tomatoes and eggs if desired. Make croutons. At serving time add the nuts, bacon, tomatoes, eggs, and croutons and toss the salad. Serve with your favorite dressing.

Note—Six sliced radishes may be added to this salad.

CROUTONS

2 slices whole wheat bread
2 T. butter or oil
¼ t. each marjoram and thyme

Toast bread and cut into ½ inch cubes. Saute in a skillet with the butter or oil and herbs for a few minutes, stirring frequently to prevent burning. Cool.

GREEN GODDESS SALAD
SERVES 4

Dressing:
1 clove garlic, minced
½ t. salt (preferably vegetable)
½ t. dry mustard
1 t. Worcestershire sauce
3 T. finely chopped chives or scallion tops (1 T. of dried green onion or leek may be used)
2 T. wine vinegar
1 cup mayonnaise
⅓ cup chopped parsley
½ cup commercial sour cream or yogurt
⅛ t. pepper (preferably freshly ground)
Salad:
1 quart mixed salad greens, washed, dried, and torn into small pieces
1 cup cooked shrimp or crabmeat
2 quartered tomatoes

Make the dressing by mixing together all the ingredients. Add ⅛ cup of this dressing to the salad greens and shrimp in a salad bowl. Garnish with tomato wedges and serve at once. Leftover dressing will keep refrigerated a week or so.

CELERY NUT SALAD
SERVES 4

5 stalks celery
1 sweet green pepper
2 tomatoes
¼ cup French dressing
½ cup grated walnuts
few leaves of lettuce

Chop the celery and green pepper and mix together. Cut the tomatoes into small wedges and add to celery mixture. Pour the French dressing over all and toss lightly. Grate the nuts on a coarse grater (not too fine). Place a leaf of lettuce on each plate, arrange celery mixture on lettuce, and sprinkle with about 2 T. of grated nuts per serving. Serve immediately.

MARINATED TOMATOES
SERVES 4

6 tomatoes
1 medium red onion (yellow onion may be substituted)
⅛ cup French dressing

Quarter tomatoes and slice onion into thin rings. Pour French dressing over the mixed tomatoes and onions in a bowl and refrigerate 1 hour. Serve as is, or on lettuce leaves.

Note—If you prefer your tomatoes without the skin, peel them. Fresh tomatoes should peel readily, but if yours don't, put them in a bowl and pour boiling water over them. Let stand for 2 minutes. Remove from water and peel.

TOMATO SAUERKRAUT SALAD
SERVES 6

1 lb. canned sauerkraut
6 medium tomatoes
3 T. oil
1 T. vinegar
1 T. catsup
1 small grated onion
1 t. raw sugar
½ t. Worcestershire sauce
6 lettuce leaves

Drain sauerkraut and pat dry on paper towels. Chop coarsely. Wash tomatoes and cut off tops. Scoop out insides and turn tomatoes upside down to drain. Chill. Chop tomato pulp and add to sauerkraut. Combine oil, vinegar, catsup, grated onion, sugar, and Worcestershire sauce. Pour over the sauerkraut and tomato mixture. Refrigerate for 30 minutes to allow flavors to blend. When ready to serve, heap sauerkraut into tomato cups and place on plates lined with a lettuce leaf.

PENNSYLVANIA DUTCH BACON SALAD
SERVES 4 TO 6

8 slices bacon
1 small onion
1 t. salt (preferably vegetable)
pinch of pepper (preferably freshly ground)
2 t. Worcestershire sauce
¼ cup cider vinegar
2 T. water
¼ cup brown sugar, packed
1 hard-cooked egg
1 head lettuce (other greens may be used)

Fry bacon till crisp. Drain on paper towels. Pour off fat leaving 3 T. in pan. Dice the onion and add to hot bacon fat. Saute till lightly browned. Add the vinegar and water (stand back from stove as you do this), then the salt, pepper, Worcestershire sauce, and the sugar. Simmer till slightly reduced in volume, about 3 minutes. Chop the hard-cooked egg and add to the sauce with the bacon. Pour hot over lettuce wedges and serve at once.

POACHED NAVEL ORANGES
SERVES 6
(GOOD WITH CHINESE FOOD)

6 navel oranges, washed
⅔ cup orange juice
⅔ cup water
⅔ cup raw sugar or honey
lettuce
watercress for garnish, if desired

Peel oranges, starting from top spirally. Go over them again removing all white membrane, as this is bitter. Cut the rind of one orange very fine. Place in a saucepan with the orange juice, water, and sugar or honey. Bring to a boil. Simmer 10 minutes. Add oranges and simmer 10 minutes, stirring frequently. Remove from sauce and refrigerate till serving time. Save the cooking liquid for fruit salads or for punch. At serving time, line plates with lettuce leaves, place an orange in center, and garnish, if desired, with watercress. Serve with mayonnaise sweetened with some of the orange syrup, if desired, using 2 T. per ½ cup mayonnaise.

ITALIAN VEGETABLE SLAW
SERVES 8

1 medium-sized head purple cabbage
1 medium onion, preferably red
6 stalks celery
1 green pepper
3 carrots
1 t. salt (preferably vegetable salt)
¼ t. pepper (preferably freshly ground)
¼ cup olive oil
1 to 2 T. raw sugar
½ cup wine vinegar
½ to 1 cup mayonnaise

Shred the cabbage. Chop the onion fine, dice the celery and pepper, and grate the carrots fine. Mix all vegetables together. Mix remaining ingredients together to make dressing and stir into vegetables.

CHINESE CUCUMBERS
SERVES 4

1 large cucumber
2 T. wine vinegar or cider vinegar
3 T. soy sauce
1 t. chopped fresh ginger root (available in
Chinese grocery stores and it may be frozen)
or one small piece dried ginger root
1 T. oil

Peel cucumber and slice thin. Add remaining ingredients and allow to marinate in refrigerator for one to two hours or longer. Serve as is.

CARROT, CELERY, AND RAISIN SALAD
SERVES 4 TO 6

½ cup raisins
4 large stalks celery
3 medium carrots
½ cup mayonnaise
lettuce leaves

Steam the raisins in a colander over boiling water for 5 minutes. Cool. Dice celery. Peel carrots and grate coarsely. Mix the carrots, celery, and raisins together. Stir in the mayonnaise. Spoon onto lettuce leaves on individual salad plates.

CHINESE CABBAGE SALAD

1 small head red or green cabbage (about one lb.)
2 T. oil
2 T. soy sauce
2 T. wine vinegar
2 T. brown sugar
½ t. salt (preferably vegetable salt)
¼ t. pepper (preferably freshly ground)
¼ t. monosodium glutamate

Cut cabbage into quarters, then into slices about ⅜ inch thick. Heat 1 T. of the oil in a frying pan and add cabbage, stirring constantly over high heat until cabbage is well coated with the oil. Don't let it soften; it should still be crisp. Remove cabbage immediately to a glass or crockery dish. Add remaining 1 T. of oil to frying pan with the remaining ingredients and when it comes to a boil, pour it immediately over the cabbage. Cover the cabbage with a plate and something to weight it down, such as a jar filled with water. Refrigerate overnight. Serve cold.

SWEET AND SOUR BEAN SPROUTS
SERVES 4 TO 6

2 cups fresh or canned mung bean sprouts
2 cups water
1 T. honey
½ t. salt
⅛ cup wine vinegar or cider vinegar
2 T. oil
2 T. honey
½ t. salt
¼ t. pepper

For instructions on sprouting see Introduction. Mung beans may be permitted to grow to 2 to 3 inches long. Bring sprouts to a boil in the 2 cups water to which the 1 T. honey and ½ t. salt have been added. Cook for 3 minutes, or 1 minute for canned sprouts. Drain. Make marinade of the remaining ingredient pour over the sprouts, and marinate overnight. Drain These will keep in the refrigerator for a couple of weeks. Serve as is, or on a salad plate garnished with lettuce.

FRUIT WREATH SALAD
SERVES 6

½ lb. green or red grapes
6 fresh apricots (or 12 canned halves)
½ cup raw sugar
2 fresh large grapefruit
1 pomegranate
3 oz. cream cheese or Neufchatel cheese
1 T. cream or milk
1 t. grated orange rind
⅓ cup chopped dates
1 bunch endive or escarole

Wash grapes and apricots (if fresh). Break the grapes into very small bunches. While grapes are still wet, dip them in some raw sugar, using about ½ cup. Allow to dry slightly on a rack while preparing remaining ingredients. Slice the grapefruit in half and section, removing the grapefruit meat from the shells. Quarter the pomegranate and remove the red seeds. Cream the cheese and add the milk or cream. Beat well. Stir in the orange rind and chopped dates. Slice the apricots in half. Place about 1 T. of the cheese mixture in the center of an apricot half and top with another apricot half. Wash and dry the endive or escarole. Arrange on a large platter in a wreath shape. Now arrange the 6 filled apricots, evenly spaced, on the green wreath. Surround the apricots with the grapefruit sections to make flowers. Arrange the frosted grapes between the apricot flowers. Sprinkle the pomegranate seeds over all. Serve immediately or refrigerate till serving time. Serve with mayonnaise.

BLUEBERRY LIME GELATIN MOLD
SERVES 6

2 envelopes unflavored gelatin
1 cup cold water
1½ cups hot water
½ cup raw sugar
½ cup lime juice, fresh or frozen
3 cups blueberries, fresh or frozen
greens

Soften gelatin in cold water for 5 minutes, using the 1 cup water. Heat the remaining 1½ cups water. Add the softened gelatin to the hot water and stir well to dissolve. Stir in the sugar. Stir well to dissolve. Cool slightly. Stir in lime juice. Chill till the consistency of unbeaten egg whites. Fold in the berries, turn into a gelatin mold or a bowl, and chill till firm. (Use a 5 cup mold.) Unmold on greens.

ORANGE PEACH GELATIN SALAD
SERVES 6

1 envelope unflavored gelatin
½ cup cold water
⅓ cup raw sugar or honey
¾ cups plus 2 T. water
¼ cup lemon juice
1 cup sliced fresh, frozen, or canned peaches
1 cup fresh orange sections (or canned mandarin oranges)
several lettuce leaves

Sprinkle the gelatin on the ½ cup cold water to soften for 5 minutes. Dissolve over boiling water. Add the sugar or honey and stir to dissolve. Add the remaining water and lemon juice. Cool slightly. Add the fruit. Turn into a gelatin mold (4 cup mold) or bowl and chill till firm. Unmold onto lettuce.

Note—Other fruits may be substituted for the peaches and oranges in this recipe, but DO NOT USE fresh pineapple, or the gelatin will not set.

MELONMINT GELATIN MOLD
SERVES 6

¼ cup raw sugar
1 cup water
3 T. finely chopped mint leaves
1 envelope unflavored gelatin
¾ cup orange juice
1 T. lemon juice
2 cups melon balls
greens

Boil sugar and ¾ cup of the water 5 minutes. Pour over mint leaves and cool, then strain. Soften gelatin in the remaining ¼ cup water for 5 minutes. Heat the orange juice to simmering and stir in the gelatin till dissolved. Cool slightly. Add the lemon juice and mint syrup. Chill till the consistency of unbeaten egg whites. Fold in the melon balls. Pour into a gelatin mold (4 cup mold) or bowl and chill till firm. Unmold on greens.

BLACK CHERRY GELATIN MOLD
SERVES 6
(GOOD WITH TURKEY)

2 1-pound cans dark sweet cherries
1 T. unflavored gelatin
¼ cup cold cherry juice
2 cups hot cherry juice
water cress or lettuce leaves

Drain cherries, reserving juice. Soften gelatin in the ¼ cup cold cherry juice for 5 minutes. Heat the remaining 2 cups cherry juice to simmer and stir in the softened gelatin till dissolved. Cool slightly. Chill till the consistency of unbeaten egg whites. Stir in the drained cherries and turn into a gelatin mold (5 cup mold) and chill till firm. Unmold onto watercress or lettuce leaves.

Note—This recipe may be made with fresh pitted cherries and bottled cherry juice. Use 2 cups cherries.

STUFFED CANTALOUPE SALAD
SERVES 4

1 small cantaloupe
2 t. unflavored gelatin
2 T. cold water
½ cup orange juice
1 T. lemon juice
2 T. raw sugar
⅛ cup fresh or frozen blueberries

Wash cantaloupe and cut a circular piece from the stem end to make a lid. Scoop out the seeds and invert melon to drain well. Soften gelatin in the cold water. Dissolve over hot water, add juices and sugar, and stir to dissolve. Cool in refrigerator till slightly thickened, then stir in berries. Fill melon cavity with gelatin mixture, replace lid and refrigerate in an upright position. It may be necessary to remove a small circular piece from the bottom of the melon so it will stand up. Cut into quarters to serve. This may also be served as a first course or as a dessert.

CRANBERRY RELISH
MAKES ABOUT 10 TO 12 CUPS
(VERY GOOD WITH TURKEY OR CHICKEN)

8 cups raw washed cranberries
3 medium oranges, quartered and seeded but with rinds left on
3 large apples, red and quartered, and peeled if desired
1½ cups honey
port wine (optional)

Prepare fruit and place about 1 cup at a time in a blender till well chopped up. Remove blended fruit and then continue blending 1 cup at a time till all fruit is used up. A food grinder may be used instead of a blender. Stir in honey and refrigerate. This will keep in the refrigerator several days, or it may be frozen. Two T. port wine may be added to each cup of relish for a different flavor.

SALAD DRESSINGS

FRENCH DRESSING
MAKES 1 CUP

2 T. wine vinegar or cider vinegar
½ cup oil
2 T. lemon juice
½ t. salt (preferably vegetable salt)
½ t. dry mustard
½ t. paprika
2 t. sugar
pinch pepper (preferably freshly ground)
¼ cup catsup
1 t. Worcestershire sauce
⅛ t. garlic powder (optional)

Mix all ingredients together in a jar and shake well.
Refrigerate. Shake before using.

BLENDER-MADE MAYONNAISE
MAKES 2 ½ CUPS

2 eggs
1 t. dry mustard
1 t. salt (preferably vegetable salt)
2 T. honey
¼ cup cider vinegar or lemon juice
2 cups oil

Break the eggs into the blender. Add the dry mustard, salt, honey, and vinegar. Add ½ cup oil. Blend. Add the remaining 1½ cups oil slowly while blending.

Note—Omit the honey if you prefer a tangy mayonnaise. Don't try to double this recipe.

YOGURT DRESSING
MAKES ¾ CUP

½ cup yogurt
¼ cup chili sauce
1½ t. wine vinegar
1 t. honey
½ t. salt (preferably vegetable salt)
dash freshly ground black pepper
pinch dry mustard
¼ t. Worcestershire sauce

Stir all ingredients together, mixing well. Store in refrigerator. Will keep two weeks.

BREADS

◦◦◦◦◦◦◦◦◦◦◦◦◦◦

Many people complain about failures with yeast dough, but actually it is quite easy to turn out delicious bread if you follow a few simple rules.

You must respect the yeast's need for the proper temperature to raise the dough. Dissolve yeast in warm water, not over 110°F. for dry granular yeast. If you use yeast cakes instead, the water should be about 95°F. One yeast cake equals one package of dry yeast.

I prefer to store all yeast in the refrigerator.

In order to raise the dough, I prefer an electric heating pad set at medium temperature.

Whole grain breads take longer to rise than white breads, but don't allow the dough to over-rise. Doughs made of 100 percent whole grains never do rise quite as high as ones made with white flour.

Also, it is very difficult to make a good bread without any wheat flour because of the relative lack of gluten in other flours. Gluten gives adhesiveness to the dough and promotes rising of the dough. Kneading also helps to make a fine grained bread.

Most breads freeze beautifully and keep in the freezer for six months to a year if properly wrapped.

WHOLE WHEAT BREAD
MAKES 4 SMALL LOAVES

1 cup scalded milk
3 T. molasses
3 T. honey
2 t. salt
4 T. oil
1 egg yolk
2 packages dry yeast
1¼ cups warm water
1 t. brown sugar
3 cups sifted unbleached white flour
½ cup wheat germ
1 T. carob flour or powder
2 T. soy flour
4 cups sifted whole wheat flour
1 egg white
2 T. water

Scald milk. Place in a blender with the molasses, honey, salt, oil, and egg yolk and blend a few seconds, or mix in a bowl with a mixer. Dissolve the yeast in the warm water with the sugar for 5 minutes. When the milk mixture has cooled to warm, add the yeast mixture. Add the sifted white flour and the wheat germ and beat 1 minute with an electric mixer. Sift the soy and carob flours with the whole wheat flour and stir into the batter. When well blended, turn dough out on a floured surface and knead 5 minutes, till smooth. Place dough in an oiled bowl, turn greased side up, cover with waxed paper and a tea towel, and let rise till doubled (about 1½ hours). Punch down and let rise again till almost doubled (about 45 minutes). Shape dough into 4 small oval loaves. Set on oiled baking sheet 3 inches apart and slash lengthwise. Cover and let rise till doubled (about 45 minutes).

Beat the egg white and the 2 T. water with a rotary beater till frothy, and brush on the loaves. Bake at 375°F. for 20 to 30 minutes till done. Cool on racks Freezes well.

Note—This dough may be baked in two 9½ x 5½ x 3-inch loaf pans. Bake 10 minutes longer.

WHOLE WHEAT RAISIN BREAD
(THIS BREAD IS ESPECIALLY SOFT FOR A WHOLE GRAIN LOAF)
MAKES 2 LOAVES

½ cup warm water
1 T. brown sugar
1 package dry yeast
1 cup sifted whole wheat flour
1½ cups water
⅓ cup honey
⅓ cup powdered skim milk
1 T. salt
⅓ cup oil
1 egg
1½ cups raisins
3½ cups sifted whole wheat flour

Mix together ½ cup warm water, 1 T. brown sugar, and 1 package dry yeast and let stand 5 to 10 minutes till puffed up. Meanwhile, place the 1 cup sifted whole wheat flour in a medium saucepan and gradually add the water. Cook over medium heat, stirring constantly, till thick. Turn out into a large bowl and add, in order, beating well by hand or with a mixer on low speed: honey, milk, salt, oil, and the egg. Place the raisins in a colander and steam over boiling water for about 5 minutes, till tender. Turn out onto a clean towel or paper towel to cool. Sift and measure remaining flour. Beat in 1 cup of the remaining flour. Stir in the softened yeast. Gradually mix in the remaining whole wheat flour with the cooled raisins. Let rest 15 minutes. Now turn out and knead for 3 to 5 minutes till satiny in texture. Place in a greased bowl, cover, place on an electric heating pad set on medium, and let rise till doubled (about 1½ hours). Punch down. Grease baking pans and press dough into them. Let rise again till doubled (about 1 hour). Bake in preheated oven at 375°F. for about 35 minutes. Cool on rack. Will freeze.

Note—The raisins may be omitted from this recipe. Also, tops may be brushed with oil and sprinkled with either sesame or poppy seeds before baking

Variation: Sprout Bread: Substitute 1 to 1½ cups sprouted wheat (which has been whirred in a blender first) for the raisins. Add a little more flour if necessary. Bake about 5 minutes longer.

See introduction for sprouting instructions.

BUTTERMILK RYE BREAD
MAKES 2 LOAVES

2 packages dry yeast
¼ cup lukewarm water
2 cups buttermilk
2 T. caraway seed
⅔ cup molasses (not blackstrap)
1½ t. salt
¼ cup oil
2 cups sifted unbleached white flour and
2 T. wheat germ
2 cups unsifted whole wheat flour
2 cups unsifted whole rye flour

Dissolve yeast in lukewarm water. Let stand 5 minutes. Heat buttermilk till lukewarm. Pour into a large mixing bowl. Add the yeast, caraway seed, molasses, and salt. Beat in the white flour and the wheat germ. Add the oil. Beat well. Gradually add the rye and whole wheat flours to form a stiff dough. Knead 5 minutes, till smooth. Put into a greased bowl, turn greased side up, cover with a piece of waxed paper and a tea towel, set on an electric heating pad set at medium, and let rise till doubled (about 2 hours). Shape into two loaves and put into greased 9 x 5 x 3-inch bread pans. Let rise till doubled while covered in pans (about 1 hour). Bake at 325°F. for about 40 minutes or till done. Turn out onto racks to cool immediately. Freezes well.

Note—This recipe may be made with sweet milk as well as buttermilk.

FRENCH BREAD
MAKES 1 LARGE LOAF OR 4 LONG ROLLS

1 package dry yeast
¼ cup lukewarm water
¾ cup hot water
2 T. oil
1 T. raw sugar
1½ t. salt
3½ cups sifted unbleached white flour
¼ cup wheat germ

Soften the yeast in the lukewarm water for 5 minutes. Combine the hot water with the oil, sugar, and salt. Cool till lukewarm. Beat ½ cup flour into the cooled water mixture. Add the softened yeast and then the wheat germ. Beat in 1½ cups flour till very smooth. Mix in enough remaining flour to make a soft dough. Turn dough out onto a lightly floured surface and allow to rest 5 minutes. Knead dough 5 minutes. Place dough in a greased bowl, turn greased side up, cover with a piece of waxed paper and a tea towel, place on an electric heating pad set at medium, and let rise till doubled, about 1½ hours. Punch down. Let rise till doubled again, about 45 minutes. Roll dough into a 14 x 8-inch oblong. Roll up tightly into a long slender loaf. Pinch ends to seal and pull to lengthen and taper. Place diagonally on a greased baking sheet sprinkled with cornmeal or flour. Make diagonal cuts at 2-inch intervals ¼ inch deep. If you wish to make rolls, divide the dough into fourths and roll out each piece into an oblong about 2 x 6 inches. Fold over so there is a crease down the center, taper ends and set on greased cookie sheet sprinkled with cornmeal. Let bread or rolls rise till doubled (about 20 to 30 minutes). Bake bread at 425°F. for 10 minutes then at 375°F. for 30 to 35 minutes, till done. Rolls should be baked at 400°F. for 15 to 20 minutes. Turn out onto racks immediately. Freezes well.

Note—½ cup soy flour may be substituted for ½ cup white flour. Bake at 25°F. less than above breads.

GARLIC BREAD

Take one loaf of French Bread (recipe just given) and slice it almost all the way through at 2-inch intervals. Mix together ½ cup soft butter, margarine, or oil with 1 t. garlic powder. Spread this mixture on the bread on both sides where you have cut through the loaf. Wrap bread in aluminum foil and heat in the oven for 15 minutes at 400°F. Serve hot.

Note—If you don't like garlic, try adding dried herbs such as ½ t. each marjoram and thyme instead of garlic.

PUMPERNICKEL BREAD
MAKES 1 LOAF

1 package dry yeast
¼ cup warm water
1½ cups milk
2 t. salt
¼ cup honey
2 cups sifted whole wheat flour
2 T. oil
2 cups sifted rye flour

Soften the yeast for 5 minutes in the warm water. Scald the milk, add salt, and cool. When milk has cooled to lukewarm, stir in the yeast, then the honey and whole wheat flour, and beat. Stir in the oil. Last, add the rye flour, mixing well. Turn out and knead well till smooth. Place in a greased bowl, greased side up, cover with waxed paper and a tea towel. Place on an electric heating pad set at medium and let rise till doubled (about 1½ to 2 hours). Punch dough down. Place in a greased 9½ x 5½ x 3-inch bread pan, cover, and let rise till doubled (about 1 hour). Bake at 350°F. for 20 minutes, turn oven down to 325°F. and bake till done, about 30 minutes more. Cool on a rack, covered with a clean thin cloth. Covering bread with a thin cloth while it is cooling makes for a softer crust. Will freeze.

Note—Four cups sifted whole wheat flour may be used in this recipe instead of 2 cups each rye and whole wheat.

WISCONSIN HARD ROLLS
MAKES 12 LARGE ROLLS

1 package dry yeast
¼ cup warm water
1 T. raw sugar
1 t. salt
¾ cup warm water
2 egg whites
3¾ cups sifted white unbleached flour or whole wheat flour
¼ cup wheat germ
2 T. oil
1 egg yolk
1 T. cold water
1 T. poppy seeds or sesame seeds

Soften the yeast in the ¼ cup warm water with the sugar and salt for 5 minutes. Then add remaining warm water. Beat the 2 egg whites till almost stiff. Sift flour, mix in wheat germ and stir 1 cup of the flour into the egg whites. Add the yeast mixture, then the oil and remaining flour. Mix well, turn out onto a floured surface and knead for about 5 minutes till smooth and elastic. Place dough in a greased bowl, turn right side up, cover with waxed paper and a tea towel, place on an electric heating pad set at medium, and let rise till doubled. This will take about 1 hour for the white flour dough and up to 2 hours for the whole wheat flour dough. Punch down and knead 2 minutes. Return to bowl and let rise again till doubled (about 45 minutes for white flour dough, longer for whole wheat). When dough has risen, form into 12 large round rolls and place on an oiled baking tray or cookie sheet about 3 inches apart. Cover and let rise till doubled. Beat the egg yolk with the 1 T. water and brush on rolls with a pastry brush. Sprinkle rolls lightly with sesame or poppy seeds. Bake at 375°F. for about 35 minutes till nicely browned. Turn out onto rack to cool immediately. Will freeze.

Note—For extra crispness, place a shallow pan of boiling water in the oven during baking of rolls.

SOY ONION ROLLS
MAKES 2 DOZEN LARGE ROLLS OR 1 DOZEN ROLLS AND 1 COFFEECAKE

1 cup lukewarm water
2 packages dry yeast
1½ cups milk
½ cup raw sugar or honey
2 t. salt
6 cups sifted unbleached white flour
1 cup sifted soy flour
½ cup wheat germ
2 eggs, slightly beaten
6 T. oil
½ cup soft butter or margarine or 6 T. oil
⅓ cup instant minced onion
2 T. poppy seed
2 T. cream or milk

Soften yeast in the ½ cup lukewarm water. Scald milk. Add sugar or honey and salt. Cool. When lukewarm, stir in the dissolved yeast. Sift flours, measure, and sift together. Mix wheat germ with the flours. Add half of the flour to milk mixture. Beat well. Add the slightly beaten eggs and the oil. Add enough of the remaining flour to make a dough that may be easily handled. Knead for 5 minutes. Put dough into a large greased bowl, turn greased side of dough up, cover with waxed paper and tea towel, set on an electric heating pad set at medium, and let rise till doubled, about 1 hour. Punch down. Let rise again till doubled (about 45 minutes). Punch down. Let rest for 10 minutes. Divide dough in half. Roll out on a floured surface to an oblong about 8 inches wide and 24 inches long. Spread the surface with half of the butter or margarine (¼ cup for each half of the dough). If you prefer, brush dough with oil instead of using the butter. Sprinkle with half of the onions and 1 T. poppy seeds. (If you are very fond of poppy seeds, you may wish to use more.) Roll up lengthwise into a long log. Cut into 2- to 3-inch pieces. Roll out the remaining half of the dough in the same manner. Fill it, roll it up and cut it into pieces. Press down the center of each roll with a knife handle to make a crease. Brush rolls with milk or cream and sprinkle lightly with remaining 1 T. of poppy seed. Place on greased cookie sheets and allow to rise till doubled (about 20 minutes). Cover them while they are rising. When doubled, bake at 375°F. for 15 to 20 minutes. Best served warm. These freeze very well.

Note—This dough may be made into bread. It will make 2 loaves. Bake in 9½ x 5½ x 3-inch loaf pans for 30 to 40 minutes.

COFFEE CAKE

Take half of the dough of the Soy Onion Roll Recipe, roll out to a 9 x 18-inch oblong. Spread with 2 T. softened butter, margarine, or oil and sprinkle with ½ cup brown sugar mixed with 2 t. cinnamon. Sprinkle with ½ cup raisins and ½ cup broken walnuts or pecans. Roll up lengthwise. Make a ring by joining the ends. Place on an oiled baking sheet. Gash with a scissor every 2 inches ⅔ of the way through on an angle. Pull dough apart a little at the gashes to expose the filling. Cover and let rise till doubled (about 45 minutes). Bake at 375°F. for 30 to 35 minutes till done. Remove to rack immediately to cool. Drizzle 2 T. honey over coffee cake while it is still warm, if desired. Coffee cake freezes well.

ANISE EASTER BUNNY ROLLS
MAKES ABOUT 12 BUNNIES

1 package dry yeast
¼ cup lukewarm water
5¾ cups sifted unbleached white flour
¼ cup wheat germ
¾ cup raw sugar
¾ t. salt
1 t. anise seed
6 medium eggs
¼ cup cold water
1 T. anise extract
½ cup oil
12 raisins

Dissolve the yeast in the lukewarm water for 5 minutes. Sift flour and mix in a large bowl with the wheat germ, sugar, salt and anise seed. Make a well in the center of flour mixture and drop in the yeast, the eggs, ¼ cup cold water, anise extract, and oil. Mix thoroughly with a spoon. Turn out and knead 5 to 10 minutes, adding a little additional flour if needed. When dough is smooth and elastic, put it into an oiled bowl, turn dough oiled side up, cover with waxed paper and a tea towel, and let rise till doubled (about 1½ hours) on an electric heating pad set at medium. Punch down. Roll out dough into a 12 x 18 x ¼-inch oblong and cut into ½-inch strips. Roll the strips between your palms to make them round. Use a 10-inch strip for the body, a 5-inch strip for the head, two 1½-inch strips for ears and a small pinch of dough for the tail. Moisten end of strip with water to make it adhere to the circle of dough for body and head. Attach head to body on top slightly to the right, using water to make it adhere. Attach ears and tail using a dab of water. Place a raisin in proper place for rabbit's eyes. Place rabbits on oiled cookie sheets, cover, and let rise till doubled (about 45 minutes). Bake at 375°F. for 15 to 20 minutes till done. Cool on rack. Bunnies will freeze.

Note—This dough may be baked in a round 10-inch tube pan at 375°F. for 4 minutes.

CHRISTMAS STOLLEN
MAKES 2 LARGE STOLLEN

1 cup milk
½ cup raw sugar
½ t. salt
1 package granular dry yeast softened in ¼ cup warm water
1 cup sifted unbleached white flour
½ cup finely cut citron
½ cup finely cut candied cherries
1 cup slivered blanched almonds
1 cup raisins (currants may be substituted for half this amount)
grated rind of one lemon (about 2 T.)
2 well beaten eggs
¾ cup soft butter
¼ t. nutmeg
3½ cups sifted unbleached white flour
½ cup wheat germ
¼ cup melted butter
½ t. cinnamon mixed with 2 T. raw sugar

Scald milk. Add the ½ cup raw sugar and salt. Cool. Soften yeast in warm water. When milk is cooled to lukewarm, add softened yeast, then the 1 cup flour, beating in with an eggbeater. Place in a large bowl, cover and set on an electric heating pad set at medium till doubled and bubbly (about two hours). Meanwhile, prepare the fruit and nuts. When dough has risen, stir in fruit and nuts, lemon rind, beaten eggs, soft butter, nutmeg, flour, and wheat germ. It may be necessary to use 1 cup additional flour while kneading dough till smooth and elastic. Roll out to two large 18 x 12-inch ovals, about ½ inch thick. Brush the stollens with the melted butter and sprinkle with the cinnamon-sugar. Make a lengthwise crease down center of dough and fold over. Remove to two large greased cookie sheets. Push into the shape of a crescent, then press edges together slightly along open edge. Brush with remaining butter. Cover with waxed paper and towel and let rise over a heating pad set at medium till nearly doubled in bulk. If you only have one heating pad you may have to raise and bake the stollens separately. When nearly doubled, bake stollens at 350°F. for 30 to 40 minutes till golden. Cool on rack. Will keep for one week if well wrapped in foil. Also will freeze.

WHITE BREAD
MAKES 2 LOAVES

1 package dry yeast
¼ cup lukewarm water
¾ cup water
1 cup milk
¼ cup powdered skim milk
2 T. raw sugar or honey
2 t. salt
2 T. oil
5¼ cups sifted unbleached white flour
¼ cup wheat germ
½ cup sifted soy flour

Soften yeast in the ¼ cup lukewarm water. Scald milk and pour into a mixing bowl. Add sugar, salt, and water. Cool. Add 1 cup of the flour, then the yeast. Stir well. Add the ¼ cup skim milk powder and the 2 T. oil. Add remaining flour and wheat germ. Turn out and let rest 10 minutes. Knead 5 minutes till smooth and elastic. Place in an oiled bowl, turn oiled side up, cover with waxed paper and a tea towel, set on an electric heating pad set at medium, and let rise till doubled (about 1½ hours). Punch down and let rise again till doubled (about 1 hour). Divide dough in half. Shape into loaves and place in greased 9½ x 5½-inch bread pans. Cover and let rise till doubled (about 1 hour) and bake at 350°F. for 40 minutes or till done. Turn out on rack immediately and cover with a tea towel.

BUTTER SUBSTITUTE SPREAD
MAKES 2 CUPS

6 T. ice water (containing crushed ice)
6 T. powdered skim milk
¾ t. salt
1½ cups oil (not olive)

Place ice water in chilled small bowl with the powdered milk and beat for about 5 minutes till stiff peaks form. Use an electric mixer at high speed. Change to low speed, add salt, and very gradually add the oil. Mix only till blended or it will gelatinize. Spoon into a pint jar and refrigerate. Use for bread, toast, pancakes, or mashed potatoes, but not for cooking.

WHOLE WHEAT MUFFINS
MAKES 9 MUFFINS

2½ T. raw sugar or honey
2½ T. oil
1 t. salt
1 slightly beaten egg
1½ cups sifted whole wheat flour
2 t. single action baking powder

Mix sugar or honey with oil. Add salt and slightly beaten egg. Sift flour, measure, and resift with baking powder. Stir into liquid mixture. Stir well to moisten flour. Bake in oiled muffin pans at 400°F. for 20 minutes. Turn out on rack immediately.

CORN BREAD
MAKES ONE 8-INCH SQUARE CORNBREAD

3½ t. single action baking powder
¾ cup sifted unbleached white flour
1 t. salt
¼ cup wheat germ
1 cup undegerminated cornmeal
1 cup milk
¼ cup oil
1 slightly beaten egg
¼ cup honey

Preheat oven to 425°F. Sift flour with baking powder and salt. Add the wheat germ and the cornmeal. Combine the milk, oil, egg, and honey and stir into flour mixture just to moisten dry ingredients. Do not beat. Turn into a greased and well floured 8-inch-square baking pan. Bake at 425°F. for about 25 minutes or till done. Cool in pan for 5 minutes, then turn out on rack and cool. Serve warm with butter.

Variation: Bacon Corn Bread: add ½ cup crisp, well drained, coarsely chopped, cooked bacon to batter.

WHOLE WHEAT BABA AU RUM

1 T. dry yeast
¼ cup lukewarm milk
2½ cups sifted whole wheat flour
½ t. salt
3 eggs
¼ cup honey
⅓ cup oil
½ cup steamed raisins
½ cup slivered blanched almonds

Sauce:

½ cup each honey, rum or brandy, and pureed peaches or apricots.

Dissolve yeast in warm milk and let sit 5 minutes. Place flour sifted with salt in deep bowl. Beat eggs with honey and oil and stir into flour. Add yeast mixture, then raisins and almonds. Knead 3 minutes. Press into an 8-inch-square pan or fancy Turk's head mold which has been well oiled. Cover and let rise till doubled on a heating pad set at medium. When doubled, bake at 350°F. for about 25 minutes till done. Remove from pan and cool on rack. When cooled, pour warm sauce over, pricking dough first all over with a fork. Although the sauce uses ½ cup rum or brandy, all the alcoholic content will have boiled off, leaving just the flavor. To make the sauce, bring the honey, rum or brandy, and pureed peaches or apricots to a boil. Simmer about 10 minutes till somewhat thickened. Cool to lukewarm before pouring over baba.

BANANA NUT BREAD
MAKES 1 LOAF

1½ cups sifted unbleached white or whole wheat flour
1¼ t. single action baking powder
½ t. baking soda
¾ t. salt
¼ cup wheat germ
1 cup mashed bananas (2 to 3)
¼ cup oil
½ cup raw sugar
2 eggs, slightly beaten
⅓ cup broken walnuts or pecans

Preheat oven to 350°F. Sift flour with the baking powder, soda, and salt. Stir in the wheat germ. Mash the bananas with a fork and measure. Beat the sugar into the oil. Add the eggs and beat well. Add half of the flour mixture, using low speed on an electric mixer, quickly add the bananas, then the other half of the flour. Do not overbeat, just mix ingredients thoroughly. Add nuts. Turn into an oiled and well floured 9½ x 5½ x 3-inch loaf pan and bake at 350°F. for about 45 minutes till done. Let stand in pan 5 minutes, then turn out to cool on rack. Will freeze.

ORANGE FRENCH TOAST
SERVES 4 TO 5

4 eggs
1 t. grated orange rind
2 T. honey
⅛ cup orange juice

2 T. Triple Sec liqueur (optional)
8 to 10 slices white or whole wheat bread

Beat eggs well and add remaining ingredients. Dip bread in this mixture, coating both sides well. Fry in hot butter on both sides till lightly browned. Serve immediately with pure maple syrup.

Variation: Add 2 T. oil to batter and toast one slice at a time in a hot waffle iron for about 3 minutes, till browned.

ORANGE DONUTS
MAKES ABOUT 4 DOZEN

3¾ cups sifted unbleached white flour
2 t. single action baking powder
1 t. baking soda
1 t. salt
¼ cup wheat germ
2 eggs
1 cup raw sugar
grated rind of 1 orange (about 1 T.)
2 T. melted butter or oil
one 6-oz. can frozen orange juice, thawed
2 T. milk
1 t. brandy or brandy flavoring
oil for frying

Sift together flour, baking powder, baking soda, and salt. Stir in wheat germ. Set aside. Beat eggs till light. Add sugar gradually, beating constantly. Blend in grated orange rind, melted butter or oil, undiluted thawed frozen orange juice, milk, and brandy. Stir in sifted ingredients. Chill for several hours. Roll out ⅓ at a time to ¼ inch thickness on a floured surface. Cut out donuts with a donut cutter. Fry in 2 inches deep hot fat (375°F.) till browned on one side (1 to 2 minutes), turn and brown on other side, remove with a slotted spoon and drain on several thicknesses of paper towels. Do not overcrowd while frying. Fry the center discs of the donuts separately as they will cook faster.

Note—Three-quarters of a cup sifted soy flour may be substituted for ¾ cup white flour in this recipe.

HOMEMADE PANCAKE MIX
MAKES ABOUT 2½ POUNDS

7 cups sifted unbleached white flour (whole wheat flour may be used)
1 cup sifted soy bean flour
½ cup wheat germ
1 T. salt
⅛ cup single action baking powder
1 cup dry skim milk

Sift flours; measure and resift all ingredients together twice to get them well blended. Store in suitable containers on your pantry shelf.

For Pancakes: Measure 2 cups mix. Add 1 t. raw sugar, 1¾ cups milk, 1 beaten egg, and ¼ cup oil. Stir together to moisten dry ingredients thoroughly. Fry on hot griddle, turning when little bubbles appear around the edge of each pancake. If desired, add 1 cup blueberries or ½ cup chopped nuts. Serve with maple syrup, jam, honey, butter, or fruit sauce. Makes about 16 pancakes.

For Waffles: Use only 1½ cups milk. Bake on waffle iron for 3 to 5 minutes till done. Makes about 6 large waffles.

For Muffins: Use 2½ cups mix, ¼ cup raw sugar, 2 beaten eggs mixed with 1 cup milk and 2 T. oil. Stir the milk, egg, and oil mixture into the dry mixture and fill greased muffin tins ⅔ full. Bake at 375°F. for 15 to 20 minutes, or till done. One half cup raisins or chopped dates or nuts may be added. Makes 12 to 15 muffins.

For Biscuits: Use 2½ cups mix. Stir together ⅔ cup milk with ⅛ cup oil. Stir into mix, roll out to ½ inch thick on floured surface, cut out with a 2½-inch round biscuit cutter and bake on an ungreased sheet at 425° F. for 10 to 12 minutes. Makes about 12 biscuits.

Note—If you have any leftovers, you may freeze them.

CAKES

I often hear complaints about cake-baking failures and when I do, I usually recommend a very simple device. I suggest the purchase of a separate oven thermometer (which should be checked first for accuracy by submersing it in boiling water to see if it reads 212°F. at sea level) to check the accuracy of the oven's thermostat. My own oven is not accurate, so without this little trick I'm sure my cakes would also flop. Of course, there are other reasons for cake failures, such as not following the recipe accurately, or improper technique. Be sure to sift dry ingredients together two to three times, cream your shortening thoroughly with the sugar, and don't overbeat batter after adding the flour.

PLAIN CAKE MADE WITH OIL
MAKES TWO 9-INCH ROUND LAYERS

3 eggs
1½ cups raw sugar
2¾ cups sifted unbleached white flour
¾ t. salt
4 t. single action baking powder
¼ cup wheat germ
½ cup oil
¾ cup milk
2 t. vanilla

Preheat oven to 350°F. Beat eggs well. Add sugar gradually and beat till light. Sift together the flour, salt, and baking powder. Stir in the wheat germ. Stir milk and oil together. Add the flour mixture and the milk mixture alternately, starting with the flour mixture and ending with the flour mixture in quarterly additions. Add vanilla. Pour into two prepared 9-inch layer cake pans. I prefer to oil the pans well first, then line with waxed paper cut to size, then oil again. Bake at 350°F. for 30 minutes or till a toothpick inserted near center comes out clean. Let stand in pans 5 minutes, then turn out on racks and peel off the waxed paper. Freezes well.

Variations: Chocolate: Add at least 6 T. cocoa, sifted mixed with 6 T. hot water. Cool slightly, then stir into batter.

Carob: Substitute 6 T. sifted carob powder for the cocoa.

POTATO FLOUR SPONGE CAKE
MAKES ONE 8-INCH SQUARE CAKE

4 egg yolks
1 T. lemon juice
1 t. vanilla
¼ cup raw sugar
½ cup potato flour (sifted)
1 t. single action baking powder
¼ t. salt
4 egg whites
⅛ t. cream of tartar
½ cup raw sugar

Preheat oven to 350°F. Beat egg yolks till thick. Beat in the lemon juice, vanilla, and ¼ cup sugar. Sift the potato flour with the baking powder and salt. Sift again. Fold into the yolk mixture. Beat the 4 egg whites till frothy, add the cream of tartar. Beat till stiff. Add the ½ cup sugar gradually. Fold the yolk mixture into the stiff whites. Put a sheet of aluminum foil into an ungreased 8-inch square pan so that it goes down one side, across the bottom, and up the other side. This is to enable you to get the cake out of the pan. Pour batter in and bake at 350°F. for about 30 minutes.

Note—Don't attempt this cake unless you have an electric mixer.

SPICE CAKE MADE WITH OIL
MAKES ONE 8-INCH SQUARE CAKE

1¼ cups plus 2 T. sifted unbleached white flour
2 T. wheat germ
¼ cup raw sugar
¼ t. baking soda
2 t. single action baking powder
½ t. each ginger, cinnamon, and cloves
1 egg, well beaten
½ cup honey
½ cup water
¼ cup oil

Preheat oven to 350°F. Sift dry ingredients together. Mix egg, honey, and water and gradually add the dry ingredients. Beat well. Prepare an 8-inch cake pan by oiling it, lining it with waxed paper, and oiling it again. Pour batter into prepared pan. Bake at 350°F. for 35 minutes or till done.

LAFAYETTE GINGERBREAD
MAKES ONE 9- TO 10-INCH TUBE CAKE

1 cup steamed raisins (optional)
3 cups sifted whole wheat flour (white flour may
be used
1 T. ginger
½ t. each cinnamon, nutmeg, and mace
1 t. cream of tartar
¼ cup powdered skim milk
½ cup brown sugar
⅓ cup oil
1 cup molasses (use half blackstrap)
⅔ cup cold black coffee
3 eggs, well beaten
grated rind and juice of a large orange
1 t. baking soda
2 T. warm water

Preheat oven to 350°F. Steam raisins in a covered
colander over boiling water for 5 minutes. Cool on a
paper towel. When cooled, take 2 T. of whole wheat
flour from the 3 cups and sprinkle it over the raisins,
coating them evenly. Sift the remaining flour with the
spices, cream of tartar, and powdered skim milk. Beat
the sugar into the oil. Beat in molasses and coffee. Beat
the eggs till light and thick. Add the dry ingredients
alternately with the eggs, starting with the dry ingredients and adding in quarterly additions. Beat in
the juice of one orange. Add the grated rind of one
orange. Dissolve the 1 t. baking soda in the 2 T. of
warm water and stir in. Add the raisins and pour batter into a prepared 9- to 10-inch tube pan. Prepare pan
by oiling, fitting it with waxed paper (do not use
waxed paper around the center hole, just oil and flour
that), and oil again. Bake at 350°F. for 1 hour, or till
done. Test with an ice pick or a long clean straw. Turn
out in 5 minutes and cool on rack.

RAISIN HONEY POUND CAKE
MAKES 1 LOAF CAKE

1 cup raisins
¾ cup chopped walnuts
2 T. flour
1 cup butter
1 cup honey
4 well beaten eggs
2¾ cups sifted unbleached white flour or whole wheat flour
2 T. wheat germ
½ t. salt
1 t. vanilla
1 t. lemon extract

Preheat oven to 300°F. Steam raisins in a covered colander over boiling water for 5 minutes. Cool raisins and chop fine. Add nuts to raisins and sprinkle both with the 2 T. flour. Cream butter with honey till fluffy. Add eggs and beat well. Sift dry ingredients together and add. Beat well. Add flavorings, then the raisins and nuts. Pour into a prepared loaf pan, 9½ x 5½ x 3. Prepare pan by oiling, lining with waxed paper, and oiling again. Bake at 300°F. for about 1 hour, or till done. Turn out on rack within 5 minutes after removing from oven.

BLENDER BANANA CAKE
MAKES ONE 8-INCH SQUARE CAKE

¾ cup raw sugar
1¼ cups sifted unbleached white flour
1 T. wheat germ
½ t. salt
1 t. baking soda
6 T. oil
3 small ripe bananas (1 cup puree)
2 eggs

Preheat oven to 350°F. Sift dry ingredients into a bowl. Place all other ingredients in a blender and blend 2 minutes till well combined. Fold into dry ingredients quickly. Pour into a prepared 8-inch square pan. Prepare pan by oiling it, lining it with waxed paper, and oiling it again. Bake at 350°F. for about 35 minutes, or till a toothpick inserted near the center comes out clean. Let stand in pan 5 minutes, then turn out on rack. Cool well before slicing.

Note—If you don't have a blender, sift dry ingredients into a bowl. Mash bananas well with a fork and mix with other ingredients in a bowl with a rotary beater. Stir into dry ingredients and bake.

CARROT CAKE
MAKES ONE 9- OR 10-INCH TUBE CAKE

2 T. wheat germ
1⅞ cups sifted unbleached white flour (or whole wheat flour)
2 t. cinnamon
2 t. baking soda
3 t. single action baking powder
1 t. salt
2 cups packed brown sugar
1 cup oil
4 eggs (well beaten)
1 cup chopped pecan nuts
2 cups finely grated carrots

Preheat oven to 350°F. Sift wheat germ, flour, cinnamon, baking soda, baking powder, and salt together. Beat the sugar into the oil. Add the dry ingredients alternately with the beaten eggs, starting and ending with dry ingredients, using quarterly additions of the dry ingredients. Fold in the nuts and carrots. Turn into a prepared 9- to 10-inch tube pan. Prepare pan by oiling it, lining it with waxed paper to fit (do not wrap waxed paper around the center hole as it may slip into the cake, but just oil and flour the center), and oiling again. Bake at 350°F. for 1 hour, or till done. Test with an ice pick if you don't have a clean straw; a toothpick won't be long enough. Turn out after cooling in pan 10 minutes, and cool on rack.

PENNSYLVANIA DUTCH CRUMB CAKE
MAKES TWO 9-INCH ROUND CAKES

3¾ cups sifted unbleached white flour
2 cups raw sugar
4 t. single action baking powder
½ t. salt
¼ cup wheat germ
1 cup butter (no substitutes)
4 eggs, separated
1 cup milk (use ¼ cup extra milk if doubling recipe)
6 T. melted butter
2 t. cinnamon

Preheat oven to 400°F. Sift flour with sugar, baking powder, and salt. Stir in wheat germ. Cut in the butter with a pastry blender or fingers till fine. Measure 1 cup of this mixture as crumbs for topping and set aside. Separate the 4 eggs. Beat egg yolks till thick, beat in the milk, and add to the remaining crumb mixture. Stir till just moistened. Beat the 4 egg whites till stiff, and fold into batter. Turn batter into two oiled and floured 9-inch round cake pans. Sprinkle top of each with half of the crumbs. Bake at 400°F. for 30 to 35 minutes, or till done. Let remain in pans 5 minutes. Turn out onto racks. While cooling, drizzle the melted butter over the cakes using 3 T. for each cake. Sprinkle with the cinnamon, using 1 t. cinnamon for each cake. Freezes well.

CHESTNUT CAKE
MAKES ONE 8- OR 9-INCH CAKE

2¼ cups vanilla sugar made from raw sugar
1½ lbs. chestnuts, in shells
4 eggs, separated
1 cup heavy cream
3 T. rum or 1 T. rum flavoring

Preheat oven to 350°F. To make vanilla sugar, place one vanilla bean sliced lengthwise in a jar with the sugar, cover and let stand at least one week. To prepare the chestnuts, cut a cross in the bottom of each chestnut. Place in a medium saucepan, cover with water, and bring to the boiling point. Take out nuts one by one and remove shell and inner skin with sharp pointed knife. Return shelled chestnuts to saucepan, cover with boiling water, cover pan, and simmer till tender (about 15 to 20 minutes). Drain. Puree in a food mill. Set aside ⅓ cup of the pureed chestnuts for topping. Separate eggs. Beat the egg yolks till thick, and gradually beat in 2 cups of the sugar. Add pureed chestnuts (except the ⅓ cup set aside) to the egg yolk mixture and fold in. Beat the egg whites till stiff and fold into chestnut mixture. Oil lightly and flour an 8- or 9-inch spring form pan. Turn batter into prepared cake pan and bake at 350°F. for 1¼ hours or till done. Cool on rack. When cooled, remove sides of pan. Beat cream till almost stiff. In order to whip cream successfully, chill bowl and beaters in freezer before whipping cream, have the cream very cold and use a small bowl. Fold remaining ¼ cup sugar, rum, and remaining ⅓ cup pureed chestnuts into whipped cream. Frost top and sides of cake with cream. Decorate with curls of solid-type carob candy. Have candy at room temperature and make curls with a vegetable peeler. Refrigerate and chill well before serving.

ITALIAN FRUIT CAKE
MAKES ONE 9- OR 10-INCH TUBE CAKE

½ cup butter
¾ cup milk
2 cups raisins
3¼ cups sifted unbleached white flour
5 t. single action baking powder
¼ t. salt
¼ cup wheat germ
½ cup softened butter
1½ cups raw sugar
5 eggs
½ cup chopped walnuts
1 t. vanilla
1 t. almond extract
1 t. lemon extract
grated rind of 1 medium orange (about 2 T.)
2 t. brandy or whiskey
1 t. anise seed

Preheat oven to 325°F. Combine ½ cup butter with the ¾ cup milk in a small saucepan and heat till butter melts. Cool. Steam the raisins in a colander over hot water, covered for 3 minutes. Cool by spreading out on a paper towel. Sift the flour with the baking powder and salt, add wheat germ. Cream ½ cup butter and beat in the 1½ cups raw sugar, then the 5 eggs, one at a time, beating well after each. Add 2 T. of the flour mixture to the raisins. Add the chopped walnuts and toss well with the flour to coat the raisins and nuts so they won't sink while baking in the cake batter. Add the sifted dry ingredients alternately with the cooled milk mixture to the creamed mixture, starting and ending with quarterly additions of the dry ingredients. Now add the vanilla, almond and lemon extract, grated orange rind, whiskey, anise seeds, and the floured raisins and nuts. Oil a 9- or 10-inch tube pan, line it with waxed paper, except center which is oiled and floured lightly, and oil again. Pour cake batter into prepared pan and bake at 325°F. for about 1 hour, or till done. Test with a clean straw or an ice pick. Cool in pan 10 minutes, then turn out and finish cooling on rack. This cake improves on standing and will keep several days.

CREAM CHEESE ICING
WILL FROST TWO 9-INCH LAYERS

1 lb. cream cheese or Neufchatel cheese, softened
½ cup honey
½ t. vanilla
grated rind of 1 orange (about 1 T.)
1 T. rum or rum extract
2 oz. grated carob candy, if desired

Cream cheese with honey in a bowl with an electric mixer. Add the vanilla, orange rind and rum. Spread on cake. Grate candy over top of cake if desired. This icing requires refrigeration.

FRUIT ICING
WILL FROST TWO 9-INCH LAYERS

3 T. arrowroot
½ cup water (cold)
¾ cup raw sugar
2 cups berries or cherries

Mix the arrowroot with the cold water. Add the sugar and ½ cup of the berries. Cook over medium heat about 2 minutes till thickened and clear. Fold in remaining berries or cherries. If you use blueberries, add 1 T. lemon juice. If you use cherries, add ¼ t. almond extract. Cool. Frost center and top of cake with this icing. For special occasions, frost the sides of the cake with whipped cream and pipe little rosettes of whipped cream around the sides or scattered all over the top. Be sure to keep refrigerated if you use the cream.

Note—This particular icing goes well with the Plain Cake Made with Oil.

FLUFFY CAROB ICING
WILL FROST TWO 9-INCH LAYERS

⅛ cup honey
2 T. water
⅛ cup carob powder
3 egg whites
pinch salt
½ t. vanilla

Combine honey, water, and carob in a small saucepan. Bring to a boil. Simmer over medium heat (238° F.) until soft balls form. While it is simmering beat the egg whites with a pinch of salt till stiff. Pour boiling mixture in a thin stream slowly over the stiff egg whites and beat steadily. When cooled to warm, beat in vanilla. Cool well before spreading on cake.

BUTTER CREAM FROSTING
WILL FROST TWO 9-INCH LAYERS

1 cup raw sugar or honey
⅛ t. cream of tartar
dash salt
¼ cup water
2 egg whites
1 t. vanilla
⅔ cup soft butter

Combine sugar or honey with cream of tartar, salt, and water in a small saucepan. Bring to a boil, reduce heat, and cook to the soft-ball stage (238°F.). Meanwhile, beat the egg whites till stiff. Beat cooked syrup in very slowly in a thin stream, beating constantly. Beat in vanilla. Cool. Cream the soft butter well and add butter 2 T. at a time to the icing beating well after each addition. This icing requires refrigeration.

Variations: Chocolate: Add 2 squares melted, cooled baking chocolate with the vanilla.

Carob: Add ½ cup sifted carob powder to finished icing.

Coffee: Add 1 T. instant coffee.

Note—The butter may be omitted from this recipe to make a boiled fluffy icing.

COOKIES AND CANDIES

Cookies take very well to whole grains, honey, and molasses. Since drop cookies are about the easiest to make, I've included several recipes for them.

RAISIN COOKIES
MAKES 5 DOZEN

1 cup water
2¼ cups raisins (preferably unsulphured)
1 t. baking soda
¼ cup oil
1½ cups raw sugar
1 t. vanilla
1 t. lemon extract
3 well beaten eggs
3¾ cups sifted unbleached white flour or
whole wheat flour
¼ cup wheat germ
2 t. single action baking powder
1 t. cinnamon
½ t. salt
¼ t. each nutmeg and allspice
½ cup walnuts, coarsely chopped
¼ cup lecithin (granular type) (optional)

Preheat oven to 375°F. Add water to raisins. Boil briskly. Cool. Add 1 t. baking soda. Cream the oil with the sugar. Add the extracts and the eggs. Sift the flour with the remaining dry ingredients. Add to batter alternately with raisins. Add nuts and lecithin. Drop by teaspoonfuls onto oiled cookie sheets and bake at 375°F. for 12 to 15 minutes till lightly browned and firm. Cool on rack. Freezes well.

HIGH PROTEIN OATMEAL COOKIES
MAKES 4 DOZEN

10 T. oil (½ cup plus 2 T.)
1 cup brown sugar (packed)
2 eggs
⅛ cup sweet or sour milk
¾ cup sifted unbleached white flour or
whole wheat flour
¼ cup sifted soy flour
2 T. brewers yeast
1½ t. single action baking powder
½ t. salt
1 t. cinnamon
¼ t. nutmeg
⅛ t. cloves
1 cup raisins
2 T. granular lecithin
¼ cup wheat germ
2¾ cups oatmeal (rolled type)

Preheat oven to 375°F. Beat the sugar into the oil. Beat in the eggs and milk. Sift the flours, brewers yeast, baking powder, salt, and spices together. Add the batter. Next add the raisins, lecithin, wheat germ, and oatmeal. Stir well. Drop by teaspoonfuls onto oiled cookie sheets and bake at 375°F. for about 10 minutes till lightly browned. Cool on rack. Freezes well.

ORANGE COCONUT
WHOLE WHEAT COOKIES
MAKES 3 TO 4 DOZEN

½ cup butter or margarine
½ cup brown sugar
½ cup honey
2 eggs
1 T. grated orange rind
2 cups finely grated coconut (preferably fresh)
2 cups whole wheat flour
½ t. baking soda
½ cup orange juice

Preheat oven to 350°F. Cream butter with sugar. Add honey, eggs, rind, and coconut. Sift flour with baking soda and add alternately with orange juice, starting and ending with flour and using ⅓ of flour for each addition. If batter seems a little thin, add a little more flour. Drop by teaspoonfuls onto lightly oiled baking sheets and bake at 350°F. for 15 minutes till lightly browned and firm. Cool on rack. Freezes well.

PEANUT SURPRISE COOKIES
MAKES 2 DOZEN

⅔ cup butter or margarine
½ cup brown sugar, packed
2 eggs, separated
1 t. almond extract
¾ cup sifted unbleached white flour
2 T. soy flour
½ t. single action baking powder
2 T. wheat germ
½ cup old-fashioned peanut butter
½ cup chopped peanuts, unsalted

Preheat oven to 350°F. Cream shortening with

71

sugar. Add egg yolk and beat well. Add almond extract. Sift the white flour with the soy flour and baking powder. Add the wheat germ to flour mixture. Stir into dough. Form into 24 small balls. Flatten each cookie ball with the bottom of a floured glass and place 1 t. peanut butter in the center of each. Wrap dough around peanut butter. Beat the egg whites till foamy and roll the cookies in the slightly beaten egg whites, then in the chopped peanuts. Place on lightly greased and floured cookie sheets and bake at 350°F. for 12 to 15 minutes till done. Cool on a rack.

CAROB BROWNIES
MAKES ONE 8-INCH SQUARE PAN OF BROWNIES

2 squares baking chocolate, melted
5 T. sifted unbleached white flour
⅛ cup sifted carob powder
1 T. sifted wheat germ
½ t. salt
½ t. single action baking powder
6 T. oil
1 cup raw sugar
2 eggs
1 cup chopped walnuts
1 t. vanilla

Preheat oven to 350°F. Melt chocolate over hot water and cool. Sift flour, measure, and resift with sifted carob powder, wheat germ, salt, and baking powder. Beat oil with the sugar and beat in the eggs one at a time thoroughly. Beat in the sifted dry ingredients, then the cooled melted chocolte, nuts, and vanilla. Turn into a prepared 8-inch square baking pan and bake at 350°F. for 30 to 35 minutes or till done. Cool in pan 5 minutes, then turn out to cool on rack. May be frozen.

MAPLE NUT DROP COOKIES
MAKES 6 DOZEN

2¾ cups sifted unbleached white flour or
whole wheat flour
1 t. single action baking powder
1 t. baking soda
1 t. salt
¼ cup wheat germ
1 cup butter or margarine
1 cup maple syrup
3 eggs
¼ cup hot water
1 cup chopped dates
1 cup chopped pecans or walnuts (or use
grated coconut)

Sift the flour with the baking powder, baking soda,
and salt. Stir in the wheat germ. Beat the maple syrup
into the softened butter. Add the eggs, one at a time.
Stir in sifted dry ingredients. Add the hot water, dates,
and chopped nuts. Chill in refrigerator several hours.
If you are in a hurry, put the dough in your freezer
for one hour. Drop from teaspoon onto oiled cookie
sheets. Bake at 350°F. for 13 to 16 minutes till lightly
browned. Cool on rack. Freezes well.

SOFT MOLASSES COOKIES
MAKES 5 DOZEN

4 cups sifted unbleached white or whole
wheat flour
½ cup wheat germ
1½ t. salt
2 t. baking soda
2 t. cinnamon
2 t. ginger
½ t. cloves
2 T. brewer's yeast
1½ cups molasses (use half blackstrap molasses)
¼ cup honey
1 cup oil
1 egg
2 T. granular lecithin (optional)

Preheat oven to 350°F. Sift together the dry ingredients. Stir the molasses and honey into the oil. Beat in the egg and gradually add the dry ingredients. Add lecithin. Beat 20 strokes. Shape into walnut sized balls with your hands which have been well floured. Bake on oiled cookie sheets at 350°F. for about 15 minutes, till lightly browned. Cool on rack Freezes well.

PUMPKIN COOKIES
MAKES 3 DOZEN

2¼ cups sifted unbleached white flour or
whole wheat flour
¼ cup wheat germ
4 t. single action baking powder
1¼ t. salt
1 t. cinnamon
¼ t. ginger
¼ t. nutmeg
¼ t. allspice
⅓ cup butter or margarine
1½ cups brown sugar
3 eggs
1 cup mashed pumpkin
½ t. orange extract
1 cup chopped pecans
1 cup currants or chopped raisins

Preheat oven to 400°F. Sift dry ingredients (except sugar) together. Cream butter with sugar. Add the eggs, one at a time, and beat well. Add the pumpkin, the orange extract, and the dry ingredients. Reserve 2 T. each nuts and currants for topping. Add remaining pecans and currants. Drop by tablespoonfuls onto oiled baking sheets. Sprinkle the cookies with the mixed pecans and currants. Bake at 400°F. for 12 to 15 minutes till lightly browned and firm. Cool on rack. Freezes well.

CINNAMON RICE FLOUR COOKIES
MAKES 4 DOZEN

2½ cups sifted rice flour
¼ t. salt
¼ t. baking soda
2 T. cinnamon
½ cup raw sugar
½ cup brown sugar
1 cup soft butter or margarine
1 egg
1 T. cream or milk

Preheat oven to 400°F. Sift dry ingredients together, except sugars. Beat the sugars into the soft butter and add the egg and cream or milk. Gradually add dry ingredients. Fill a cookie press and press onto oiled cookie sheets. Bake at 400°F. for 10 to 12 minutes. Cool on rack.

PRESS COOKIES MADE WITH OIL
MAKES 6 DOZEN

1 cup oil
1 cup raw sugar
3 eggs
1 t. almond extract
3¾ cups sifted unbleached white flour
¼ cup wheat germ
3 t. single action baking powder
¼ cup milk

Preheat oven to 350°F. Beat the sugar and the oil together. Add the eggs one at a time and mix thoroughly. Add almond extract and mix well. Sift the flour with the wheat germ and baking powder. Add half of the dry ingredients into the creamed mixture.

Add the milk. Beat well. Add the remaining dry ingredients gradually. Allow mixture to set 10 minutes. Pack into cookie press and press onto ungreased cookie sheets. If desired, sprinkle tops of cookies with blanched slivered almonds. Bake at 350°F. about 15 minutes, till lightly browned. Cool on rack.

NUT CRISPS
MAKES 3 DOZEN

1½ cups ground nuts (almonds, walnuts, or filberts)
½ cup butter
⅓ cup raw sugar
pinch salt
1 t. vanilla

Grind nuts fine in a blender ⅓ cup at a time. Grate them if you don't have a blender. Cream butter and sugar. Stir in ground nuts, salt, and vanilla. Form dough into a long roll 1 inch in diameter. Wrap in waxed paper and chill several hours or overnight till firm. Set oven to 350°F. Cut into ¼-inch slices and bake 7 minutes on ungreased baking sheets, or till lightly browned. Cool on paper towels on racks to absorb excess grease.

CHOCOLATE COVERED RAISINS
MAKES 1½ CUPS

¼ cup honey
4 1-oz. squares baking chocolate
1½ cups raisins, dates or nuts
1½ t. vanilla

Melt honey with the chocolate over boiling water. When chocolate is melted, remove from hot water

and cool to 95°F. or 100°F. At this point, add 1½ t.
vanilla. Stir well. Drop the fruit or nuts in, coat well
on all sides, and drop by teaspoonfuls onto waxed
paper. Keep refrigerated.

Variation: Carob dipped nuts or fruits. Melt 6 oz.
solid carob candy over hot water. Add 2 T. butter.
Cool. Dip at same temperature. Refrigerate.

APRICOT COCONUT BALLS
MAKES ONE DOZEN

¾ cup dried apricots or peaches (preferably
unsulphured)
½ cup walnuts
¾ cup grated coconut (preferably fresh)
1 t. grated orange rind
1 T. lemon juice

Put apricots or peaches, nuts and coconut through
a food chopper. If you have no food chopper, chop
them fine. Combine with remaining ingredients and
shape into balls.

CAROB COCONUT EASTER EGGS
MAKES ABOUT 2½ POUNDS

3 cups raw sugar
1 cup water
¼ t. cream of tartar
¼ cup cold firm butter (no substitutes)
1 t. vanilla
¼ cup butter
2 cups grated coconut
10 oz. solid-bar-type carob candy

In a 2-quart saucepan, which has a heavy bottom,
mix the sugar, water, and cream of tartar together.

Bring to a boil and cook over moderate heat to 240°F. (soft-ball stage). Wash sides of pan with a brush in hot water to prevent crystals from forming in candy. Pour candy onto damp baking tray (or onto a marble slab if available) and cool to lukewarm, about 110°F. Break the ¼ cup butter into small pieces and place on candy with the vanilla. Work with a spatula back and forth with a pushing motion till thick and cool, about 10 minutes. Knead 1 to 2 minutes. Knead in 2 cups finely grated coconut (preferably fresh). Shape into large, medium, or small eggs. Let stand on waxed paper for 30 minutes to dry. If you find the candy is a little soft, chill it in a freezer for about 1 hour. Then shape and return it to freezer for about 1 hour till the eggs are frozen hard. When ready to dip candy, melt carob candy with the ¼ cup butter over hot water. Let cool to about 95°F. for dipping. Dip the candy, using a spoon or a fork, coating all sides. If you are dipping frozen candy, you may need to reheat the carob mixture. Place on waxed paper to dry. If desired, sprinkle eggs, before carob has set, with some lavender-colored sugar made by mixing ½ T. grape juice with ⅛ cup raw sugar. Refrigerate candy and let ripen for 2 days before eating.

Variation: Orange coconut eggs: Use 1 T. orange extract in place of the 1 t. vanilla.

PRALINE KISSES
MAKES ABOUT 40 TO 50 CANDIES
(APPROXIMATELY 1½ POUNDS)

2 cups dark brown sugar
¼ cup water
¼ cup butter or oil
1½ cups broken pecan halves
¾ cup wheat germ

Combine the brown sugar with the water and butter or oil. Stir well in a medium saucepan. Bring to a boil, reduce heat to low and cook till firm-ball stage (248°F.). Remove from heat and stir in the nuts and the wheat germ rapidly. Drop by tablespoonfuls onto waxed paper and cool. Will freeze.

SESAME SEED CANDY
MAKES ABOUT 1¼ POUNDS

1½ cups raw sugar or brown sugar
½ cup honey
2 T. water
¼ t. cinnamon
1 T. lemon juice
1 cup sesame seeds, preferably lightly toasted

Sesame seeds are often packed already toasted, but if yours aren't, sprinkle them out on a shallow baking tray and bake at 350°F. for about 5 minutes, stirring around every couple of minutes. Remove from oven and taste to see if they are toasted enough to develop a flavor. Cool. Mix sugar, honey, and water in a heavy-bottomed small saucepan and bring to a boil. Reduce heat and simmer 25 to 35 minutes, till 300°F. (hard crack stage). Add cinnamon, lemon juice, and sesame seeds. Pour into an oiled 8 x 8-inch square pan and cool till hard. Turn out and break into small pieces with a knife handle or a small hammer.

CAROB PEANUT CANDY
MAKES ABOUT 24 PIECES

6 oz. solid-bar-type carob candy
½ cup old-fashioned peanut butter
1 cup shelled peanuts

Melt the carob candy in top of a double boiler over hot water. When melted, stir in the peanut butter. When mixture is well blended and peanut butter is melted, stir in the peanuts. Drop by teaspoonfuls onto waxed paper. Chill till set. Refrigerate.

HALVAH
MAKES ABOUT 12 PIECES

1 cup ground sesame seeds
¼ cup honey
¼ cup almond extract (optional)

Mix all ingredients together till consistency is creamy but not sticky, adding more honey or sesame seeds if necessary. Form into small balls by rolling between your hands. Store in refrigerator if kept for any length of time.

ICE CREAM AND SHERBETS

∞∞∞∞∞∞∞∞∞∞∞∞∞

STRAWBERRIES LA RUSSE
SERVES 4

juice of ½ orange
¼ cup Triple Sec liqueur
1 qt. strawberries or raspberries (fresh or
frozen)
1 pt. homemade vanilla ice cream
1 cup heavy cream, whipped (may be omitted)

Pour liqueur and orange juice over the washed
and stemmed berries. Refrigerate for ½ hour to allow
flavors to blend. At serving time, beat ice cream with
a spoon to soften it slightly. Whip the cream till stiff
and fold into ice cream. Pour over berries and stir.
Serve immediately.

HONEY ICE CREAM
SERVES 6

1 T. unflavored gelatin
¼ cup water
½ cup honey
2 cups light cream or top milk (or substitute
1 cup heavy cream for 1 cup of the light cream)
1 cup evaporated milk
2 t. vanilla

Soften gelatin in cold water. Mix together in a heavy-bottomed saucepan the honey and 1 cup of the light cream or top milk. Bring to simmering. Stir. When honey is dissolved, add the softened gelatin and stir to dissolve. Add the remaining 1 cup light cream, the 1 cup evaporated milk, and the vanilla. Pour into freezing trays and freeze till mushy. Beat with a mixer till softened. Refreeze.

Variations: Rum Raisin: Soak ⅓ cup raisins in 3 T. rum and add when you beat the partially frozen ice cream.

Carob: Add ½ cup carob syrup when beating ice cream (recipe given in Beverages section).

Fruit: Add 2 cups crushed fruit when beating. Omit vanilla. ¼ t. almond extract is good with peaches.

Banana: Mash 4 bananas with 2 T. lemon juice and add when beating. Omit vanilla.

For Easter: Shape hardened ice cream into egg shapes and roll in lavender-colored coconut (colored with grape juice). Refreeze.

MOLASSES PARFAIT
SERVES 6

4 egg yolks
1 cup molasses (not blackstrap)
2 cups heavy cream
1 cup minced pecans

Beat the yolks and stir in the molasses. Cook over hot (not boiling) water till thickened, whisking or stirring constantly. Cool. Fold in the cream which has been whipped. Fold in pecans. Freeze, preferably in individual fancy cups.

Variation: Maple: Substitute 1 cup maple syrup for molasses.

BLUEBERRY SHERBET
SERVES 4 TO 6

½ cup blueberries, fresh or frozen
juice of 1 lemon
juice of 1 orange
⅓ cup honey
2 cups milk

Sieve or blend blueberries in a blender. If using frozen berries, partially thaw them. Add remaining ingredients and blend together. Pour into freezing tray and freeze till mushy. Beat with a mixer till smooth and return to freezing tray to refreeze.

ROSE PETAL SHERBET
SERVES 4 TO 6

1 cup rose petals (packed slightly for measuring)
2 T. raw sugar
1 cup raw sugar
1 pt. boiling water
1 cup orange juice (preferably fresh, unstrained)

Make sure the roses have not been sprayed. Wash them after measuring and chop fine. Add the 2 T. sugar and crush into the rose petals. Dissolve the 1 cup sugar in the pint of boiling water. Stir in the rose petals, bring to a boil, and simmer, without stirring, for 10 minutes. Cool. Add orange juice. Turn into freezing tray and freeze till mushy. Then beat till smooth and refreeze.

DESSERTS

∞∞∞∞∞∞∞∞∞∞∞

APPLE BROWN BETTY
SERVES 4 TO 6

¼ cup melted butter, margarine, or oil
1¼ cups lightly toasted whole wheat bread cubes
⅓ cup wheat germ
3 thinly sliced apples
½ cup brown sugar
¼ t. nutmeg
½ t. cinnamon
grated rind and juice of ½ lemon
⅔ cup raisins (optional)

Preheat oven to 350°F. Stir butter into bread cubes. Cover bottom of a buttered baking dish (6 x 11 inches or approximately 8 x 8 inches) with a layer of the bread cubes. Sprinkle lightly with the wheat germ, layer with the sliced apples, and sprinkle with part of the sugar, spices, lemon rind, juice, and raisins if used. Repeat these layers once, covering top with a light layer of bread cubes and wheat germ. Bake at 350°F. for 30 to 35 minutes covered (use a piece of foil if necessary). Remove cover and bake 10 minutes longer till browned. Serve with light cream.

FIGS IN WINE
SERVES 4

12 canned figs
1 cup fresh or frozen strawberries
2 sliced bananas
½ cup sweet wine

Mix fruit together and pour wine over all. Refrigerate ½ hour to let flavors blend. Serve as is or with sour cream sauce.

SOUR CREAM SAUCE
MAKES 1 CUP

Mix together 1 cup sour cream with 2 T. vanilla sugar. Make vanilla sugar by mixing ½ of a vanilla bean, split lengthwise, with 1 cup raw sugar. Let sugar stand at least one week. (Yogurt may be used in place of sour cream.)

WARM SPICED APPLE DESSERT
SERVES 4

5 to 6 apples
1 cup sifted unbleached white flour
½ cup brown sugar
2 T. wheat germ
½ t. cinnamon
¼ t. nutmeg
½ cup butter or margarine

Preheat oven to 350°F. Slice apples thinly. Place in the bottom of a buttered casserole (approximate size, 8 x 8 inches) to thickness of approximately 3 inches. Cover with topping made of remaining ingredients.

Desserts

Mix sifted flour with remaining ingredients and cut
the butter or margarine into the dry ingredients with
a pastry blender or fingers till fine. Bake at 350°F. for
30 to 40 minutes uncovered. Serve warm with light
cream if desired.

BRANDIED PINEAPPLE
COTTAGE CHEESE MOLD
SERVES 6

½ cup of the juice from the pineapple
1 T. unflavored gelatin
1 egg yolk
¼ cup light brown sugar (packed)
¼ cup raw sugar
1 T. lemon juice
½ T. grated orange rind
½ cup orange juice
1 cup cottage cheese
1 T. brandy or brandy flavoring
1 egg white
1 cup canned crushed pineapple (preferably
packed in its own juice with no sugar)

Soak the gelatin in ¼ cup of the pineapple juice for
5 minutes. Mix the egg yolk in a saucepan with the
sugars, lemon juice, orange rind, remaining pineapple
and orange juices. Heat thoroughly, stirring constantly.
Stir in the softened gelatin. Cool. Sieve the cottage
cheese and fold in with the brandy and the crushed
pineapple. Chill till thick. Beat egg white till stiff
and fold into cheese mixture. Pour into a fancy gelatin
mold and chill well.

DRIED FRUIT COMPOTE
SERVES 4

⅔ cup dried figs (preferably unsulphured)
1 cup pineapple juice
½ cup dried apricots (preferably unsulphured)
½ cup dried pears (preferably unsulphured)

Remove stems from figs. Bring pineapple juice to a boil and add the fruit. Cover and simmer till tender, 5 to 10 minutes. Remove from heat and chill in refrigerator before serving. May be served as a dessert or as a breakfast fruit.

APPLESAUCE WITH RAISINS
SERVES 6

10 medium apples (about 2½ lbs.)
1½ cups water
⅔ cup honey
1 t. cinnamon
½ t. nutmeg
½ cup raisins

Peel, core, and quarter apples. Cook in the water, covered, till tender, about 10 minutes. Puree in a food mill. Add remaining ingredients and simmer 2 minutes. Chill before serving.

APPLEBERRY SAUCE
SERVES 6 TO 8

10 medium apples (about 2½ lbs.)
1 to 1½ cups water (depending on juiciness of fruit)
2 cups berries (blueberries, strawberries, raspberries, cranberries, peaches or apricots)
⅔ cup honey (more for cranberries)

Peel, core, and quarter apples. Place in medium saucepan with water, berries, and honey and bring to a boil. Cover and simmer about 10 minutes till done. Puree in a food mill. Taste for sweetening. To intensify peach or apricot flavor, if used, add ¼ t. almond extract. Chill.

NEW ENGLAND BIRD'S NEST PUDDING
SERVES 6

6 medium apples (about 2 lbs.)
2 cups raw sugar or 1½ cups honey
1 cup water
2 cups cream
2-inch piece of vanilla bean, split lengthwise
(or substitute 2 t. vanilla)
¼ cup raw sugar or honey
3 eggs, beaten

Set out a shallow 1½ qt. baking dish (about 10 x 6 inches). Heat 1 qt. water for boiling-water bath for pudding. Wash and core, but don't peel, 6 medium apples. Combine in a deep saucepan 2 cups raw sugar, or 1½ cups honey, with 1 cup water and bring to a boil. Add apples, cover, and reduce heat. Simmer till barely tender (about 7 minutes). Remove with a slotted spoon to a baking dish. Save the syrup to make applesauce. Scald 2 cups light cream with a 2-inch piece of vanilla bean which has been split lengthwise. Remove some of the black specks in the center of the vanilla bean with the tip of a knife and stir into cream. While cream is scalding, beat 3 eggs slightly. Add ¼ cup raw sugar or honey. Now slowly stir in the hot cream. Strain through a sieve over the apples. Remove the pieces of vanilla bean to the custard and apples. Set baking dish in a larger one filled with boiling water. Bake at 350°F. for 40 to 60 minutes till knife comes out clean when inserted in custard. When cooled, refrigerate for at least 2 hours before serving.

Note—2 t. vanilla extract may be substituted for the vanilla bean. Add it to the egg mixture.

STIR AND ROLL PIE CRUST
MAKES ONE DOUBLE 9-INCH CRUST

1¾ cups sifted unbleached white flour
1 t. salt
¼ cup wheat germ
½ cup oil (not olive)
5 T. milk

Sift the flour with the salt. Stir in the wheat germ. Mix the oil with the milk and stir into flour mixture. When well blended, turn out onto waxed paper and cut dough in half. Cover with another sheet of waxed paper to roll, unless you have a stocking on your rolling pin. Roll out other half of dough. Line your pie pan with dough, fill, and cover with other crust. Bake according to pie recipe. Do not refrigerate or freeze this crust before baking.

For a single crust pie, cut the recipe in half. Prick the crust all over with a fork and bake at 450°F. for 10 to 12 minutes till lightly browned.

CHERRY BERRY PIE
MAKES ONE 9-INCH PIE

1-lb. can water-packed pie cherries
10-oz. package thawed frozen strawberries
(You may substitute 1 pt. home frozen sweetened thawed strawberries. If you use unsweetened berries, you will need more sugar.)
¾ cup raw sugar
¼ cup arrowroot
1 T. lemon juice
pastry for double 9-inch pie crust

Preheat oven to 425°F. Drain fruits and measure the juices. You should have 1 cup. Add water if necessary. Mix arrowroot with sugar. Stir in 1 cup of the fruit juices. Cook over medium heat, stirring constantly, till thick and clear, about 5 to 8 minutes. Remove from heat and add fruit and lemon juice. Cool before filling pie shell. Line a 9-inch pie pan with pastry, pour in filling, arrange top crust in place. Fold the top crust over and under the edges of the lower crust and press together. Flute crust between forefinger and thumb or press with fork prongs against pie pan. Slit top crust to allow for steam escape. Place in preheated oven and bake at 425°F. for 25 to 30 minutes. If the edges of the pie crust seem to be browning too readily, wrap them in a 2-inch strip of aluminum foil. Cool on a rack.

PEAR HONEY ANISE PIE
MAKES ONE 9-INCH PIE

5 almost-ripe Bosc or Bartlett pears
½ cup honey
3 T. arrowroot
1 t. whole anise seeds
grated rind of 1 lemon (about 1 T.)
pastry for double crust 9-inch pie
1 T. lemon juice
1 T. butter or margarine

Preheat oven to 425°F. Peel the pears and cut into ¼-inch slices. Drizzle the honey over the pears and toss well to coat pears. Mix the arrowroot with the anise seeds and lemon rind. Sprinkle over pears and mix lightly. Place the pears in pastry-lined pie pan. Sprinkle pears with lemon juice and dot with the butter or margarine. Adjust top crust, fold the top crust over and under the lower crust and press together. Flute edges. Slit top. Bake at 425°F. for 45 to 50 minutes. Cool on rack.

BLUEBERRY APRICOT PIE
MAKES ONE 9-INCH PIE

2 cups fresh blueberries, or 2 cups partially defrosted frozen blueberries
2 cups fresh apricot halves (Canned apricots may be substituted. If packed in syrup, reduce sugar by ½ cup.)
1¼ cups raw sugar
4 T. arrowroot
½ t. cinnamon
2 T. butter or margarine
pastry for double crust 9-inch pie

Desserts

Preheat oven to 425°F. Wash fruit. Combine sugar, arrowroot, and cinnamon. Sprinkle over combined fruit and toss lightly. Place fruit mixture in a pastry lined 9-inch pie tin, dot with butter or margarine. Adjust top crust. Fold top crust over and under the lower crust and press together. Flute edges. Slit top. Bake at 425°F. for about 40 minutes. Cool on rack.

MANGO PIE
MAKES ONE 9-INCH PIE

Filling:
¾ cup raw sugar
1½ cups water
¼ cup lemon juice
3 ripe mangoes
2 T. water
2 T. arrowroot
2 T. butter

Mix sugar, 1½ cups of water, and lemon juice in a saucepan. Boil 5 minutes. Peel and slice mangoes ¼ inch thick. Drop mango slices into sugar syrup, reduce heat and simmer 2 minutes. Cool. Drain slices and set syrup aside. Stir the arrowroot with the 2 T. water. Stir this into the cooled syrup. Add the butter and cook over medium heat till thickened and clear. Remove from heat and cool. Make up crust.

Graham Crust:
1 cup graham cracker crumbs
(Use 100 per cent whole wheat grahams available in health food stores.)
¼ cup melted butter, margarine, or oil

Break graham crackers (about 6) into a blender and blend till in crumbs. Or, roll the crackers with a rolling pin between 2 sheets of waxed paper. Mix crumbs with melted butter, margarine, or oil and press into a 9-inch pie shell. Chill a few minutes. When syrup is cooled, arrange half of the mango slices in the crust, cover with syrup and arrange remaining mango slices on top. Chill.

ITALIAN CHEESE PIE
MAKES ONE 9-INCH PIE

Pastry:
1¾ cups sifted unbleached white flour
½ t. salt
¼ cup wheat germ
⅝ cup cold butter
2 T. sherry wine

Filling:
3 cups ricotta or cottage cheese
1 t. vanilla
4 eggs
½ cup honey

Preheat oven to 350°F.

Crust: Sift flour with salt. Add wheat germ. Cut in the butter till fine, leaving a few larger pieces of butter. Stir in sherry. Add a little water if necessary. Roll out half of dough to fit a 9-inch pie pan. Roll out remaining half and cut into ½-inch strips for lattice top.

Filling: Place all ingredients in blender and blend till smooth (about 1 minute). Or, sieve the cheese and beat in remaining ingredients. Pour into pastry-lined pie pan. Place lattice strips criss-cross on top. Pinch edges of lattice strips to rim of pastry. Bake at 350°F. for about 45 minutes till firm, but not dry. Test pie by putting a silver knife in filling near center. It should come out clean. Cool on rack. Store in refrigerator.

SWEET POTATO PIE

1¼ cups riced cooked sweet potatoes
½ cup honey
¼ cup sugar
¼ t. ginger
1 t. cinnamon
½ t. salt
2 egg yolks, slightly beaten
1 T. molasses, not blackstrap
2 egg whites, stiffly beaten.
½ cup pecan halves (optional)
1 9-inch pastry shell, unbaked

Preheat oven to 450°F. Combine the mashed sweet potatoes with the honey, sugar, and seasonings. Stir the beaten egg yolks into the milk. Add the molasses and stir into sweet potato mixture. Beat the egg whites till stiff and fold into sweet potato mixture. Turn into unbaked pie shell. Sprinkle with pecan halves and bake at 450°F. for 15 minutes, then at 350°F. for about 20 minutes till done. A silver knife inserted near the center should come out clean when pie is done.

STRAWBERRY RHUBARB PIE
MAKES ONE 9-INCH PIE

stir-and-roll pie crust
¼ cup arrowroot
1 cup raw sugar
2 cups halved strawberries
1½ cups diced (approx. ⅜-inch dice) rhubarb
1 T. butter

Preheat oven to 425°F. Make up pie crust first and line 9-inch pie pan with half of it. Mix arrowroot with sugar and add fruit, stirring gently. Pour into pastry-lined pan, dot with the 1 T. butter broken into small bits and top with remaining rolled out pastry. Turn under and flute edges and make opening in top for steam. Bake at 425°F. for 20 minutes, then at 350°F. for 30 minutes. Cool on rack.

PUMPKIN PIE
MAKES ONE 9-INCH PIE

single crust for 9-inch pie shell
⅔ cup brown sugar
½ t. salt
2 t. pumpkin pie spice or 1 t. cinnamon, ½ t. ginger, ¼ t. cloves, ¼ t. allspice, and 1 t. grated orange rind (optional)
2 whole eggs or 4 egg yolks
1 cup light cream or half milk and half cream
1½ cups strained pumpkin, canned or homemade

Preheat oven to 425°F. Roll out crust, line a 9-inch pie dish with it, and bake at 425°F. for 5 minutes to harden the crust slightly and prevent pumpkin filling from soaking in. Mix sugar with salt and spices. Beat eggs lightly and add cream gradually. If pumpkin is very moist, use less cream. Add pumpkin to cream mixture, then stir in sugar mixture. Pour into pie shell and bake at 425°F. for 15 minutes, then at 300°F. 40 to 50 minutes or till knife comes out clean when inserted near center. Cool on rack. Pumpkin pie will not freeze after it is baked. Commercially, freezing is done by adding chemicals, but you may make up extra filling and freeze it in quart containers before baking, thaw out completely, and bake like a fresh pie.

MEAT AND MAIN DISHES

SPAGHETTI AND MEATBALLS
SERVES 4 TO 6
(WITH ENOUGH SAUCE LEFTOVER FOR ANOTHER MEAL)

Sauce:
MAKES ABOUT 1½ QTS.

¼ cup olive oil
3 cloves garlic, chopped fine
3 chopped onions, preferably red onions
3 T. chopped parsley (2 T. dried parsley
may be used)
2 qts. stewed or canned tomatoes, preferably
Italian style
3 T. dry white wine
2 t. salt (preferably vegetable salt)
½ t. pepper (preferably freshly ground)
1 t. dried oregano
¼ cup chopped mushrooms, if desired
2 small cans tomato paste

Heat oil, add garlic and onions, and saute 10 minutes over medium heat, stirring frequently till tender. Add parsley, tomatoes, wine, salt, pepper, and oregano. Stir well. Cover and cook over low heat 2 hours. Add mushrooms and cook covered 1 hour. Add tomato paste and cook uncovered 1 hour. Force mixture through a sieve or food mill. Taste for seasoning. Refrigerate when slightly cooled. The sauce is better the next day. It will freeze, but it loses some of its flavor. If you freeze it, add a little garlic powder when reheating.

Meatballs

½ cup wheat germ
¼ cup milk
½ lb. ground beef or ground round steak
2 T. chopped parsley (1 T. dried parsley may be used)
¼ t. garlic powder
2 T. Parmesan cheese, grated
1 egg
1 t. salt (preferably vegetable salt)
¼ t. pepper (preferably freshly ground)
2 T. olive oil

Soak the wheat germ in the milk for 5 minutes. Add other ingredients and form into 12 medium meatballs. Fry in about 2 T. olive oil for about 5 minutes on each side. If desired, break up the balls to make loose meat. Add to hot spaghetti sauce and simmer 15 to 30 minutes. While the meatballs are simmering in the sauce, prepare the spaghetti. Bring 3 qts. of water and 1 T. of salt to a boil in a very large pot. When water is boiling violently, add 8 oz. high protein spaghetti. Cook over high heat, stirring occasionally with a slotted spoon to prevent any spaghetti from sticking to bottom of pan, till done (about 5 to 10 minutes). See package for exact time. If spaghetti threatens to boil over, just add 1 T. oil. When done, add 1 cup cold water to stop boiling. Drain immediately in colander. It is not necessary to rinse the spaghetti in the colander if you cooked it in the large quantity of water as recipe recommends. Serve immediately, covering with the meatballs and sauce. Pass grated Parmesan cheese to sprinkle over spaghetti and sauce if desired.

BAKED BEANS MADE WITH OIL
SERVES 6

2 cups dried pea beans
1½ qt. warm water
¼ cup oil
¼ cup reserved bean liquid
¼ cup chopped raw bacon
¼ cup catsup
¼ cup chopped onion
1 t. salt (preferably vegetable salt)
¼ cup molasses (not blackstrap)
½ t. dry mustard
6 frankfurters, if desired

Soak beans in the warm water overnight. (Or boil them for 2 minutes in the water, remove from heat, and soak 1 hour.) Boil the soaked beans in the same water for about 45 minutes, until they begin to soften. Drain, reserving liquid. Mix ¼ cup of the bean liquid with the remaining ingredients (except frankfurters). Place in a bean pot and pour enough bean liquid over the beans to just cover them. Cover bean pot and bake at 250°F. for 6 to 7 hours, adding a little bean liquid if necessary. Remove lid during the last hour to permit browning. If desired, cut the frankfurters into 1-inch chunks, place on top of beans, and bake uncovered at 350°F. for 20 minutes. Beans will freeze well.

Note—Hot water may be substituted for bean liquid if necessary.

MEAT-STUFFED POTATOES

4 large baking potatoes
2 T. oil
1 onion, chopped
½ to 1 lb. ground beef or ground round steak
½ t. salt
¼ t. pepper
¼ cup catsup

Bake potatoes 40 to 50 minutes at 400°F. till tender. Heat oil in a skillet and brown onion for 2 minutes. Add meat and cook till done. Pour off any excess fat. Add salt, pepper, and catsup. Slice potatoes in half lengthwise, scoop out the insides, and mash them in a bowl with a fork. Add 2 T. butter or margarine if desired. Add the potatoes to the meat mixture and refill the potato shells with the potato-mixture. Reheat in oven for 5 to 10 minutes.

MEAT CRUST PIE
SERVES 4

1 lb. ground beef or round steak
½ cup rolled oats
¼ cup wheat germ
½ t. salt
½ t. oregano
⅛ t. pepper
½ cup milk
1 egg
one 10-oz. package frozen mixed vegetables, cooked
2 cups hot mashed potatoes

Mix all ingredients together, except the vegetables and potatoes. Line bottom and sides of a 9- or 10-inch pie pan with meat mixture and bake at 350°F. for 40 minutes. When meat is done, pour off any excess grease, fill center with cooked, frozen mixed vegetables and garnish around edge of pie with globs of the mashed potatoes. Reheat in oven for 5 minutes.

MEATBALL VEGETABLE STEW
SERVES 6

1 lb. ground beef or round steak
2 T. chopped onion
2 T. chopped green pepper
¼ cup wheat germ
1 t. salt
1½ t. dry mustard
1 t. chili powder
½ cup milk
1 egg, slightly beaten
2 T. oil
2 T. flour
2 cups tomato juice
3 potatoes
6 carrots
1 chopped onion
1 t. salt

Mix first nine ingredients and shape into 12 balls. Roll each in flour and brown well in 2 T. oil. Place in a 2-qt. casserole. Brown 2 T. flour in the skillet and add 2 cups tomato juice. Simmer till thickened, stirring constantly. Remove from heat. Prepare the vegetables. Peel and quarter the potatoes, cut the carrots into 1-inch chunks and chop the onion. Add the salt, then the vegetables to the tomato sauce. Pour all over meatballs and stir around to mix the meatballs in the sauce. Cover and bake at 350°F. 1½ hours till carrots are tender.

LIVER BOURGEOIS
SERVES 4

1 lb. liver (any kind)
⅛ to ¼ cup wheat germ
6 slices bacon
1 small minced onion
1 small minced green pepper
⅓ cup catsup
1 t. Worcestershire sauce
salt and pepper

Slice liver into ½-inch slices and roll in wheat germ. Fry bacon till crisp. Drain on paper. Pour off all but 3 T. drippings. Saute the minced onion and pepper in the bacon fat for 2 minutes. Add the liver and brown 5 minutes. Add the catsup and Worcestershire sauce and simmer until liver is done (about 1 minute). Add crumbled bacon and salt and pepper if needed.

BARBECUED BEEF KIDNEY
SERVES 4

one 1¼-lb. beef kidney
2 sliced onions
2 T. oil
1 cup water
3 T. vinegar
½ cup catsup
2 T. Worcestershire sauce
1 t. salt
¼ t. chili powder

Wash kidney, remove outer membrane. Split through center, remove fat and tubes, and cook covered 15 minutes at 15 lbs. pressure in a pressure cooker, or simmer 2 hours. Drain. Brown onions in oil. Add 1 cup water and remaining ingredients. Cover and simmer 30 minutes. Add kidney and simmer 20 minutes.

HEART PATTIES
SERVES 4

1 lb. beef heart
1 medium onion (optional)
1 t. salt
¼ t. pepper
flour
3 T. oil

Remove veins and fat from beef heart. Grind the heart in a meat grinder (or use your blender). Mix in the finely chopped onion, salt, and pepper. Roll the heart, made into 4 patties, in flour and saute in hot oil till done. Serve with catsup.

Note—These may be baked in a moderate oven for 20 minutes instead of frying.

BURGUNDY MEAT LOAF
SERVES 4

1 lb. ground beef or round steak
¾ cup oatmeal (rolled type)
2 T. bacon-flavored brewers yeast (optional)
3 T. finely chopped onion
1 egg
pinches of rosemary, thyme, and oregano
½ cup burgundy wine

Mix all ingredients together and bake in an oiled casserole or 9½ x 5½ x 3-inch bread pan for 45 to 60 minutes.

SPRINGTIME LAMB PATTY STEW
SERVES 6

4 slices bacon
approximately 1½ lbs. lamb patties (6 patties)
one medium onion, diced
12 new potatoes (1½ to 2 lbs.), peeled and
halved or quartered
6 medium carrots, scraped and cut into
½-inch slices
3 whole cloves
1½ t. vegetable salt
¼ t. black pepper, preferably freshly ground
1½ cups water
1½ cups diced celery
1½ cups shelled fresh peas (approximately 1½ lbs.
in shells, frozen peas may be substituted)
2 t. chopped fresh or frozen mint

Dice bacon and fry in a skillet till crisp. Drain and
set aside. Pour off all but 2 T. bacon drippings and
fry the lamb patties till browned on both sides. Pour
off excess fat from lamb. Add diced onion and saute
lightly for 2 minutes. Add peeled potatoes, cut in
halves or quarters depending on size; carrots, scraped
and cut into ½-inch slices; 3 whole cloves; salt; pepper;
and water. Bring to a boil. Reduce heat, cover, and
simmer 10 minutes. Add diced celery and peas and
cook 10 to 15 minutes longer till just tender. Remove
the 3 cloves. Sprinkle with crisp bacon and chopped
mint and serve.

HERBED ROAST LEG OF LAMB
SERVES 6 TO 8

one 6-lb. leg of lamb
2 T. olive oil
½ t. garlic powder
1 t. salt (preferably vegetable salt)
½ t. pepper (preferably freshly ground)
2 t. rosemary
1 cup dry white wine
½ cup water

Place lamb in a roasting pan without rack. Rub lamb with the olive oil, then sprinkle on the garlic powder, salt, pepper, and rosemary. Pour the wine mixed with the water around the lamb and bake uncovered at 325°F. for about 3 hours, basting occasionally.

BAKED SLICED HAM WITH APPLES
SERVES 4

2 large ½-inch thick slices of ham (about
1½ lbs.)
1 t. dry mustard
2 t. vinegar
2 large cooking apples
½ cup brown sugar
1 T. oil

Remove bone from ham. Mix mustard and vinegar. Spread the mixture thinly on the ham slices. Slice apples very thin (about ⅛ inch thick) and spread them on the ham slices. Sprinkle the apples with the brown sugar. Roll ham up lengthwise, rolling fat sides into the center. Hold together with skewers. Rub the ham rolls with the oil, place in a shallow baking pan, and bake uncovered at 375°F. for 40 minutes.

VEAL SCALLOPINI
SERVES 4

1 small onion, chopped
1 lb. boneless veal cutlet, cut into 2-inch
square pieces
2 T. olive oil
1 clove garlic, minced
1 cup tomato sauce
½ t. salt (preferably vegetable salt)
¼ t. pepper (preferably freshly ground)
¼ t. oregano, dried
⅛ t. basil, dried

Saute onion and meat in hot olive oil till lightly
browned on both sides. Add remaining ingredients
and simmer, covered, 20 to 30 minutes, till veal is
tender.

VEAL PARMIGIANA
SERVES 4

Sauce:

2 cloves garlic, minced
1 onion, finely chopped
3 T. olive oil
1 t. salt (preferably vegetable salt)
¼ t. pepper (preferably freshly ground)
1 cup tomato sauce
2½ cups stewed or canned tomatoes
½ t. oregano

Meat:

> 1 egg
> ¼ cup or more wheat germ
> ¼ cup grated Parmesan cheese, or more if needed
> 1 lb. veal cutlet, cut very thin
> 2 T. olive oil
> ½ lb. sliced sharp cheddar cheese (Mozzarella cheese may be used)
> ¼ cup grated Parmesan cheese
> ¼ t. oregano, finely crumbled

Make sauce first by sautéeing garlic and onion in hot olive oil till golden (about 5 minutes). Add remaining ingredients, breaking up the tomatoes slightly, and bring to a boil. Simmer uncovered 20 minutes.

Meanwhile, prepare meat and preheat oven to 350°F. Beat egg in a shallow bowl. Mix wheat germ with ¼ cup Parmesan cheese in another shallow bowl. Cut meat into serving-sized pieces (about 2 x 3 inches). Dip veal in beaten egg first, then in wheat germ-cheese mixture. Saute till golden brown on both sides in the hot olive oil in a skillet. Set browned veal in an oiled 12 x 8 x 2-inch baking dish. Slice cheese thin and arrange ⅔ of it on the veal. When sauce is done, pour ⅔ of it over the cheese. Arrange remaining cheese on top, cover with remaining sauce, and sprinkle with the ¼ cup grated Parmesan cheese and ¼ t. finely crumbled oregano. Bake uncovered at 350°F. for 30 minutes.

CHINESE GROUND STEAK WITH ONIONS
SERVES 4

1 lb. ground round steak (ground beef may be substituted)
3 T. soy sauce
2 T. sherry wine (optional)
1 t. raw sugar
½ lb. onions, sliced (about 3 medium onions)
6 water chestnuts
3 T. oil
½ t. salt (preferably vegetable salt)
¼ t. pepper (preferably freshly ground)
1 T. arrowroot dissolved in 2T. cold water

Mix ground steak with soy sauce, sherry, and sugar. Slice onions and water chestnuts. Heat oil in frying pan, add onions, and fry for 2 minutes, stirring constantly. Add salt and pepper. Add meat and fry 2 minutes while stirring. Add water chestnuts, cover, and simmer 10 minutes over lower heat. Mix arrowroot with water, add to meat mixture, and cook 1 to 2 minutes till thick and glazy.

VEGETABLE MEAT LOAF
SERVES 4

1 lb. ground beef or round steak
1 egg
½ t. salt (preferably vegetable salt)
¼ t. pepper (preferably freshly ground)
¼ cup wheat germ
one 10-ounce can condensed vegetarian vegetable soup

Mix all ingredients together and pack into an oiled casserole or loaf pan (9 x 5 x 3 inches) and bake at 350°F. for 1 to 1¼ hours.

SPINACH AND MUSHROOM
STUFFED PORK CHOPS
SERVES 6

one 10-oz. package frozen chopped spinach
(or 1½ cups fresh cooked spinach)
1 small onion, chopped
1 4-oz. can mushrooms, chopped and drained
½ t. salt (preferably vegetable)
¼ t. black pepper (preferably freshly ground)
¼ t. grated nutmeg (preferably freshly grated)
6 double pork chops with pocket cut in
2 cups chicken stock (don't use bouillon cubes)

Cook the spinach and drain well. If you use fresh
spinach, chop it finely. Add chopped onion, chopped
mushrooms, salt, pepper, and nutmeg. Stuff the pork
chops with the spinach filling. Close with toothpicks.
Place in a shallow pan, pour the chicken stock over
all, and bake at 375°F. for 2 hours, uncovered, basting occasionally with the chicken broth. Remove
chops from broth and, if desired, garnish with peach
halves, dark sweet cherries, and water cress.

CHINESE PORK CHOPS WITH TOMATO AND LETTUCE
SERVES 4

6 to 8 pork chops
3 T. oil
2 t. salt (preferably vegetable salt)
1 cup canned tomatoes (or diced fresh tomatoes)
2 cups celery, cut into ½-inch slices
½ cup sliced onions
2 cups sliced lettuce
1 cup water
2 T. catsup
¼ cup Worcestershire sauce
4 t. sugar
1½ t. monosodium glutamate
¼ t. pepper (preferably freshly ground)
2 T. arrowroot mixed with ⅛ cup water

Heat 1 T. of the oil in a large frying pan, add pork chops, and fry over moderate heat till done. Remove pork chops and cut into 1-inch pieces, removing bones. Prepare vegetables. Add remaining 2 T. oil to frying pan, then add salt, tomatoes, sliced celery, onions, and lettuce and stir constantly while frying for 2 minutes over high heat. Add water, cover, and cook 1 minute. Add meat, cover, and cook 1 minute. Add catsup, Worcestershire sauce, sugar, monosodium glutamate, and pepper and stir well. Mix arrowroot with ⅛ cup water and stir into mixture in frying pan. Cook 1 to 2 minutes till thick and glazy.

ORIENTAL ROAST BEEF
SERVES 6 TO 8

One 4-lb. pot roast of beef

MARINADE:

> 2 medium sliced onions
> ¼ cup hot water
> ⅛ t. ginger powder
> ¼ cup soy sauce
> ¼ t. garlic powder

Mix all ingredients for marinade together. Brown the meat in hot oil (about 2 T.). Turn and brown on all sides. Pour marinade over meat, cover, and bake at 350°F. for about 2½ hours, till tender. Thicken gravy with 1 T. arrowroot mixed with 2 T. cold water if desired. Cook over burner on medium heat.

BAKED STUFFED ROUND STEAK
SERVES 4

> one 1½-lb. thin round steak
> 10 sliced mushrooms (fresh, canned, or frozen)
> one medium onion, sliced thin
> ¼ cup wheat germ
> 3 T. oil
> ½ cup Burgundy wine (red)
> ½ cup beef stock
> 1 to ½ t. salt (preferably vegetable)
> ¼ t. pepper
> 1 chopped onion

Cut off excess fat from steak. Pound till thin (about ⅝ of an inch). Spread the steak with the sliced mushrooms and the sliced onion and sprinkle the wheat germ over all. Drizzle the oil over all. Roll up lengthwise and tie with string firmly in several places. Roll in flour and brown in about 2 T. hot oil. Turn and brown all sides evenly. Add to the meat the wine, beef stock, salt, and pepper. Add the chopped onion. Cover and bake at 350°F. for 1½ to 2 hours, till tender. Remove cover last ½ hour of baking time to brown somewhat.

SPICY BEEF BRATEN
SERVES 6 TO 3

one 4-lb. pot roast of beef
3 cups beef stock
1 t. ground sage or poultry seasoning
½ t. ground thyme
1 t. salt (preferably vegetable salt)
½ t. black pepper (preferably freshly ground)
2 t. whole cloves
2 bay leaves (crumbled)
2 T. grated lemon rind
3 T. lemon juice
2 T. oil
1 medium carrot cut into 1-inch chunks
1 medium onion, sliced

Combine beef stock with all the seasonings, the lemon rind, and the lemon juice. Bring to the simmering stage. Pour hot over the meat which you have placed in a small crock or a large bowl (not metal). When slightly cooled, refrigerate for 24 hours, turning meat in marinade several times. Remove meat from marinade and reserve. Brown the meat well in the 2 T. oil. Add the sliced carrot and onion and brown slightly. Pour the marinade over all and bake at 350°F. for 2½ hours till meat is tender. If you wish to serve gravy, strain the marinade and thicken with

1 T. arrowroot mixed with 2 T. cold water. Cook till thick over medium heat on stove. Serve with mashed potatoes.

CRUSTED ROAST VEAL
SERVES 6

one 3-lb. roast of veal
small clove garlic
¾ cup chicken stock
¼ cup white wine

Crumb Crust:

2 T. chopped onion
2 T. oil
1 cup wheat germ
½ cup grated Parmesan cheese
2 T. dried parsley
½ t. salt
pinch basil
pinch black pepper (preferably freshly ground)
for garnish if desired
one 8-oz. can mushroom caps and parsley

Rub the meat with the peeled clove of garlic. Discard garlic. Add the wine to the chicken stock and pour it over the meat in a roasting pan. Cover and bake at 350°F. for 2 hours or till veal is tender. Remove meat from pan.

Make crust: brown the onion in the oil for 2 minutes, stirring frequently. Add the remaining ingredients. Brush meat with the drippings from the pan and roll in the crumb mixture. Drizzle on 2 T. of the drippings from the pan. Place on a rack set on a shallow pan and bake at 350°F. for 20 minutes or till golden. For garnish, if desired, heat an 8-oz. can of mushroom caps in some of the broth. Surround meat with the mushroom caps and garnish with parsley.

SUKIYAKI
SERVES 4 TO 6

½ cup sliced onions
6 stalks celery
½ lb. fresh spinach
½ lb. fresh mushrooms (Frozen or canned
may be substituted, a 4-oz. can will do.)
5 scallions
1-lb. round steak (partially frozen for easy
slicing)
3 T. oil (not olive oil)
⅓ cup beef stock
1 T. soy sauce
1 t. salt (preferably vegetable salt)
¼ t. pepper (preferably freshly ground)
¼ t. monosodium glutamate

Slice onions and celery (cut the celery on an angle
in ½-inch slices). Wash spinach and remove stems.
Dry. Chop spinach coarsely. Slice mushrooms and
scallions. Cut meat into thin slices (about ½ x 2
inches). Heat oil in skillet. Saute meat till browned
on all sides. Add vegetables and saute while covered,
5 minutes, stirring frequently. Combine the beef stock,
soy sauce, salt, and seasonings. Mix well. Cover and
simmer 10 to 15 minutes till vegetables are tender,
but still slightly crisp. If desired, thicken with 1 T.
arrowroot mixed with 2 T. cold water. Stir into
sukiyaki and cook 2 minutes over medium heat till
thickened.

CHINESE ROAST PORK
SERVES 6

1 cup soy sauce
½ cup sherry wine
½ t. garlic powder
one 4-lb. pork loin

Mix together all ingredients except pork. Place pork in a deep bowl, pour marinade over it, and let stand 2 hours, turning occasionally. Place in roasting pan and bake, covered, with the marinade at 375°F. for uncovered ½ hour.

ITALIAN CHICKEN LIVERS
SERVES 4

1 lb. chicken livers, cut in half
¼ cup olive oil
2 cloves garlic, minced
½ cup canned or stewed tomatoes
⅓ cup red wine such as Burgundy

Brown the chicken livers in oil. Add remaining ingredients, cover, and simmer 30 minutes. Remove cover and simmer a few minutes to reduce the sauce somewhat.

CHINESE CHICKEN LIVERS
SERVES 4 TO 6

1 lb. sliced chicken livers
⅓ cup dry white wine
⅓ cup oil
½ cup chicken stock
2 slices fresh Chinese ginger, or ½ t. ginger powder
2 T. soy sauce
1 t. salt (preferably vegetable salt)
½ cup sliced bamboo shoots (canned)
½ cup sliced water chestnuts (canned)
2 minced scallions

Pour half of the wine over the sliced liver and let marinate 5 minutes. Heat oil in frying pan and fry liver, stirring 1 minute. Add remaining ingredients and cook 1 to 2 minutes more till liver is done. If desired, thicken with 1 T. arrowroot mixed with 2 T. water and cook till glazy.

POULTRY

Since both chicken and turkey are comparatively low in calories and saturated fat, they are ideal entrees for weight watchers and people trying to reduce the saturated fat content of their diets. Chicken also lends itself well to various types of recipes, so you can serve it often without it becoming boring to the palate.

OVEN FRIED CHICKEN
SERVES 4

one 2- to 3-lb. frying chicken, cut up
⅛ to ½ cup evaporated milk
1 cup wheat germ
1 t. salt (preferably vegetable salt)
¼ t. pepper (preferably freshly ground)

Roll the cut-up chicken in the evaporated milk. Mix the wheat germ with the salt and pepper. Roll the chicken parts in the wheat germ mixture and place on a baking tray covered with a sheet of aluminum foil (to save scouring later) and bake at 350°F. for 1 hour, turning once. This may be served cold for picnic lunches as well as hot for dinner.

COUNTRY CAPTAIN
SERVES 4

one 2½- to 3-lb. frying chicken, cut up
salt, pepper, and flour
2 T. oil
1 finely chopped onion
1 chopped green pepper
1 clove garlic, finely minced
¾ t. salt (preferably vegetable salt)
dash pepper (preferably freshly ground)
1½ t. curry powder
¼ t. thyme
2 cups canned or stewed tomatoes
1 t. chopped parsley (or ½ t. dried parsley)
2 cups cooked brown rice
⅔ cup blanched, slivered almonds
2 T. oil
1 T. arrowroot
2 T. cold water
3 T. currants (raisins may be substituted if
necessary)

Skin chicken parts. Roll in flour and sprinkle with
salt and pepper. Brown in 2 T. oil (using more if
necessary) in skillet on all sides. Remove from skillet.
Add the chopped onion, pepper, and garlic to skillet
and cook very slowly, stirring constantly for 5 minutes.
Add salt, pepper, curry powder, thyme, tomatoes, and
parsley. Heat thoroughly. Place chicken in a roasting
pan, pour sauce over all, cover, and bake at 350°F.
for 45 minutes or till tender. While chicken is cooking,
prepare the rice. I prefer to cook rice in the top of a
double boiler over simmering water so that I can
cook it in a minimum amount of water and yet not
have to worry about it burning. Use 2 cups boiling
water, ½ t. salt, and ⅔ cups raw brown rice. Mix

together in the top of a double boiler. Stir occasionally. It will take about 40 minutes to cook till tender. Drain off any excess water. (You shouldn't have any, but just in case you do, drain it off.) Season with 3 T. butter or margarine. Keep over the hot water to keep it warm. Prepare the almonds. To blanch the almonds, cover them with water in a small pan, bring to a boil, and simmer 2 minutes. Drain, rinse with cold water, and slip off the brown skins. Cut into lengthwise slivers (about 6 per almond). Saute the almonds over low heat in the 2 T. oil in a small saucepan till lightly browned. Salt lightly. If desired, the almonds may be toasted on a shallow tray in the oven for 5 to 10 minutes at 350°F., stirring frequently till a golden color. When the chicken is done, remove it from the sauce and keep warm in the oven on a platter. Mix the arrowroot in the 2 T. cold water and stir into the sauce. Cook over moderate heat, stirring constantly, till thickened. Stir in the currants. Place rice in the center of a platter, surround with the chicken, and pour the sauce over the rice. Sprinkle the almonds over all.

HAWAIIAN CHICKEN
SERVES 8

1 cup drained, canned crushed pineapple (preferably packed in juice without sugar syrup)
¼ cup lemon juice
2 T. honey
2 T. soy sauce
1 t. salt
¼ t. pepper (preferably freshly ground)
¼ t. ginger
4 chicken breasts, or 8 to 10 chicken legs

Combine all ingredients and pour over the chicken in a shallow baking pan. Bake at 375°F. for about 1 hour basting frequently, and turning once, till tender.

ORIENTAL CHICKEN
SERVES 4

one 2½- to 3-lb. frying chicken, cut up

Marinade:

1½ T. wine vinegar
½ t. paprika
¼ t. rosemary
½ t. monosodium glutamate
1 t. salt (preferably vegetable salt)
⅛ t. pepper (preferably freshly ground)
½ t. raw or brown sugar
¼ t. garlic powder
3 T. soy sauce
½ t. Chinese bead molasses (regular molasses may be substituted)
6 T. oil

Beat all ingredients for marinade together with a rotary beater. Pour over the chicken pieces in a bowl and refrigerate for 24 hours, turning chicken occasionally. Place chicken in a roasting pan with the marinade and bake at 350°F. for 1 hour, uncovered, basting occasionally. Remove chicken pieces from sauce to serve. If you serve this dish with rice, you may serve 1 T. of the pan drippings over each serving of rice.

CORN BREAD STUFFING FOR CHICKEN OR TURKEY
WILL STUFF A 10-LB. BIRD

1 cup chopped celery
¼ cup chopped parsley
1 small onion, chopped
6 T. oil
8 cups corn bread crumbs (recipe given with
Breads)
½ t. thyme
1 t. salt (preferably vegetable salt)
¼ t. pepper (preferably freshly ground)
6 slices bacon, fried, drained, and crumbled
1 cup chopped pecans (optional)

Brown the celery, parsley, and onion in the oil for
5 minutes. Add remaining ingredients and stuff bird
loosely. If you have any extra stuffing, you may bake
it in a package of aluminum foil for 1 hour.

BREAD STUFFING FOR CHICKEN OR TURKEY
MAKES 1 QT. FOR A 4-LB. CHICKEN

3½ cups good quality, firm white bread cubes or
pieces
⅓ cup oil
¼ cup minced onion
½ cup chopped celery (use a few inside leaves)
½ cup wheat germ
1 t. salt (preferably vegetable)
½ t. thyme
¼ t. pepper (preferably freshly ground)
½ t. sage
¼ t. poultry seasoning (or more if desired)
2 T. chopped parsley, if desired (1 T. dried
parsley may be used)

Cube or tear bread into proper size cubes or pieces, preferably with no pieces over 1-inch square. Saute onion in the oil for 5 minutes over moderate heat till limp and yellow. Add celery and saute for 5 minutes more, stirring frequently. Mix the bread with the wheat germ, seasonings, and parsley. Pour the cooked onion and celery over bread mixture and mix well. If you like a moist stuffing, add 2 T. water or broth. Stuff bird loosely.

ROAST CHICKEN OR TURKEY

Wash bird inside and out. Sprinkle inside of bird with salt if desired. Stuff bird loosely. Truss the opening with skewers and string. Tie the legs together and tie the wings to the body if they are spreading out. Place bird on a rack on a baking tray or roasting pan. Pat bird dry. Brush the bird lightly all over with oil and place breast side up on tray. Cut a piece of double-thick cheesecloth to fit over the top of the bird. Dip it in hot water, wring it out, dip it in oil and place it over breast of bird. Bake bird according to chart listed below. When breast is slightly browned (about the middle of baking period), turn bird to permit underside to brown. Cover underside with cheesecloth. During last ½ hour of baking time, remove cheesecloth, turn breast side up, and allow breast to brown a little more. Remove from oven a few minutes before serving so that it will carve easier.

TO COOK GIZZARD, LIVER, OR HEART

Wash gizzard, heart, and liver and cook in water to cover, seasoned with ½ to 1 t. salt (preferably vegetable salt), ¼ t. pepper (preferably freshly ground), ¼ t. poultry seasoning, 2 slices onion, and 1 sprig parsley. Cook over moderate heat till tender. Remove the liver in 15 to 20 minutes and cook gizzard and heart about 20 minutes more. Strain broth and save.

CHART FOR ROASTING POULTRY
ROAST ALL BIRDS AT 325°F.

Turkey

4 to 8 lb.	3 to 4 hours
8 to 12 lb.	4 to 4½ hours
12 to 16 lb.	4½ to 5 hours
16 to 20 lb.	5½ to 7 hours
20 to 24 lb.	7 to 8½ hours

Chicken

4 to 5 lb.	2½ to 3 hours
over 5 lb.	3 to 4 hours

Duck

4 to 6 lb.	3½ to 4 hours

TURKEY CHOW MEIN
SERVES 4

¼ cup oil
2 cups leftover turkey pieces
2 cups celery, cut into ½-inch diagonal slices
1 cup Chinese Snow Peas (also called sugar peas)
(these peas are used IN the shells)
½ cup water chestnuts, sliced
4-oz. can mushrooms (or ½ lb. fresh or frozen
mushrooms, sauteed for 2 minutes)
2 cups fresh or canned bean sprouts, drained
2 t. salt (preferably vegetable salt)
¼ t. monosodium glutamate
½ t. garlic powder
1 cup chicken stock (do not use bouillon cubes)
¼ cup arrowroot combined with 1 c. cooled
chicken stock

Heat oil. Saute turkey for 1 minute. Add vegetables,
seasonings and 1 cup chicken stock. Cover skillet and
simmer 10 minutes, till vegetables are tender, but
still slightly crisp. Mix arrowroot with remaining
chicken stock, stir in, and cook till thickened. Serve
with cooked brown rice.

Note on Snow Peas—Snow peas are difficult to ob-
tain. I find it necessary to grow my own and freeze
them in order to have them for my Chinese dishes.
If you can't find them, just omit from recipe.

DUCKLING WITH SAUERKRAUT
SERVES 4

1 Long Island duckling, about 3 to 4 lbs.
2 T. oil (approximately)
one pound of sauerkraut, fresh or canned
one 6-oz. can frozen orange juice concentrate
2 T. arrowroot
2 T. cold water

Cut duckling into quarters and remove the fat and skin. Discard. Brown the duckling in the 2 T. of hot oil. Add the sauerkraut with its juice, the orange juice concentrate, and cover. Simmer 45 minutes. Mix arrowroot with water. Stir into duck dish and simmer till thickened.

This is really a delicious dish, even though it sounds very odd. The sauerkraut seems to cut the fat of the duck, and the orange juice sweetens the sauerkraut.

TURKEY CREOLE
SERVES 4 TO 6

2 cups turkey broth left from cooking the giblets
(or use chicken stock made by adding 2 T.
chicken base to 2 cups hot water)
2 cups canned tomatoes
¼ cup chopped green pepper
½ cup chopped onion
⅓ cup chopped celery
1 t. vegetable salt
1 t. raw sugar
one small bay leaf
⅔ cup uncooked brown rice
2 cups diced cooked turkey

Combine all ingredients in a large saucepan, bring to a boil, cover, and simmer till rice is tender, about 30 minutes. Remove bay leaf and serve.

SEAFOOD

OYSTER-STUFFED STRIPED BASS
SERVES 6

Stuffing:

6 slices toasted good white bread
4 slices bacon
2 T. oil
¼ cup wheat germ
3 sprigs parsley, chopped
1 scallion, chopped
1 t. salt (preferably vegetable salt)
¼ t. pepper (preferably freshly ground)
½ t. dry mustard
1 T. lemon juice
18 oysters with their liquor

Fish:

one 6-lb. striped bass, cleaned
6 slices bacon
2 lemons
1 onion
1¼ cups dry white wine
½ cup chopped parsley

Make stuffing: Toast bread and cut into small cubes (about ½-inch square). Fry the bacon till crisp. Drain on paper towel and then crumble the bacon. Discard bacon fat. Heat the 2 T. oil in skillet and saute the chopped scallion for 2 minutes. Add to bread cubes with crumbled bacon. Stir in the wheat germ, seasonings, and last, the oysters, tossing lightly.

Stuff fish with stuffing and fasten opening with toothpicks. Put extra filling in an aluminum foil pouch and bake separately with the fish. Place fish in a roasting pan, cover with the 6 slices of raw bacon. Slice lemon and onion thin and place over the fish. Pour wine over all and sprinkle with the chopped parsley. Cover and bake at 325°F. for 1½ hours.

POACHED SALMON STEAKS
SERVES 4

1½ T. oil
⅛ cup diced celery
1 small carrot, cut into 1-inch pieces
1 small onion, quartered
1 small bay leaf
2 peppercorns
1 clove
2 sprigs parsley
¼ t. rosemary
2 t. salt
¼ of a lemon
3 cups water
4 salmon steaks (4 to 6 oz. each)

Heat oil. Saute celery, carrot, and onion for 5 minutes. Add seasonings, lemon, and water. Simmer in a small saucepan, covered, for 30 minutes. Strain. Return to medium saucepan or skillet and add salmon steaks. Simmer 7 to 10 minutes or till fish flakes with a fork. Remove with a slotted spoon or spatula to keep fish whole. May be served hot or cold. If served cold, serve with mayonnaise and a parsley garnish.

TUNA OR BONITA FISHCAKES
SERVES 6

¼ cup oil
½ cup flour, unbleached white or whole wheat
1½ cups milk
2 T. dried minced onion
¼ cup minced parsley (or use 2 T. dried parsley)
¼ cup lemon juice
¼ t. pepper (preferably freshly ground)
two 7-oz. cans tuna or bonita fish flakes, drained
½ cup wheat germ
salt to taste (preferably vegetable salt)
wheat germ for coating (about ¾ cup to 1 cup)
oil for frying

Heat oil in a medium saucepan. Add the flour. Blend well and gradually add the milk. Cook till thickened. Add the onion, parsley, lemon juice, pepper, fish, and wheat germ. Taste for salt. I find additional salt unnecessary, as the fish is usually quite salty. Mix well. Spread out on a shallow dish or pan and refrigerate for several hours. Shape into patties and roll in the wheat germ. In a skillet, heat oil to ½-inch depth to 375°F. and fry fish cakes till well browned on both sides (about 2 minutes on each side). Drain on paper towels. Serve with catsup.

Note—These may be baked in a 400°F. oven on an oiled baking sheet for about 20 minutes. Turn once. These will freeze and may be reheated in a 400°F. oven for a few minutes.

CHINESE BAKED FLOUNDER
SERVES 6 TO 8

one 4-lb. flounder
¼ cup soy sauce
¼ cup oil
2 T. chopped parsley
2 T. lemon juice

Place washed fish in a baking dish. Mix together remaining ingredients and pour over fish. Bake at 350°F. till done, about 20 to 30 minutes. The fish will flake with a fork when done. Place on serving platter carefully with a large pancake turner and garnish with parsley or watercress. Other fish may be baked in the same manner.

FLORENTINE FLOUNDER
SERVES 6

2 cups chopped cooked spinach (one 10-oz. package frozen chopped spinach)
2 lbs. flounder fillets
2 T. minced onion
1 clove garlic, finely chopped
dash pepper
½ t. salt (preferably vegetable)
3 T. lemon juice
1 t. Worcestershire sauce
¼ cup oil

Cook spinach and drain well. Wash and dry flounder. Mix the minced onion, garlic, salt, and pepper with spinach. Spread spinach mixture over fish fillets and roll up lengthwise, jelly roll fashion. Fasten with toothpicks and place in an oiled shallow baking dish. Mix together the lemon juice, Worcestershire sauce, and oil and pour over fish. Bake at 400°F. for 25 minutes, or till fish flakes with a fork.

HALIBUT STEAK WITH OLIVES AND ALMONDS
SERVES 6

¼ cup blanched and slivered almonds
⅛ cup oil
2 t. dry mustard
2 T. wine vinegar
¼ cup sliced ripe olives
2 lb. halibut steak

Blanch almonds by simmering them in water to cover for 3 minutes. Drain and slip off brown skins. Sliver. Heat oil and saute the almonds till golden, stirring constantly over moderate heat (about 3 minutes). Add remaining ingredients except fish. Arrange fish steaks in a shallow oiled baking dish. Pour sauce over fish and bake at 350°F. for 20 to 25 minutes.

SHRIMP SUPREME
SERVES 6

3 lbs. raw shrimp
½ cup oil
¼ cup sherry
½ cup finely chopped onions
¼ cup chopped parsley
1 clove garlic, minced
1 chopped raw mushroom or one 4-oz. can sliced mushrooms
3 fresh tomatoes, peeled and diced, or 1 cup canned tomatoes
1 cup beef stock, preferably made from beef stock base
1 t. chili powder
1 t. salt, preferably vegetable salt
¼ t. pepper

Wash and peel shrimp; remove the black veins. Heat oil in a skillet, add shrimp, reduce heat, and saute till lightly browned, stirring occasionally. Add remaining ingredients, cover, and simmer for 20 to 30 minutes. Serve with rice.

BAKED COD, HALIBUT, OR FLOUNDER
SERVES 4

1 lb. cod halibut, or flounder fillets
¼ t. salt
⅛ t. pepper
1 small onion, sliced
½ lemon, thinly sliced
½ cup catsup
3 T. sherry wine
1 T. oil

Place fish fillets in a shallow baking dish. Sprinkle with salt and pepper. Arrange onion and lemon slices on top. Mix catsup, sherry, and oil. Pour over fish. Bake at 375°F. for 30 to 40 minutes.

BROILED SHRIMP
SERVES 6

2 lbs. fresh or frozen shrimp
2 t. salt
½ bay leaf
1 t. whole peppercorns
1 t. curry powder
¼ cup wine vinegar
3 T. white or sherry wine
1 cup French dressing (recipe given in salad
    section)

Wash shrimp. Place in a large saucepan and add water to cover (about 1½ qt.). Add remaining ingredients (except French dressing). Bring to a boil. If you like, add a few caraway seeds to take away odor. Turn down heat and simmer 10 minutes. Drain shrimp, shell, and devein. Place shrimp in a bowl, cover with French dressing, stir around, cover, and refrigerate for one hour or longer. Drain shrimp from dressing and broil 2 to 3 minutes on each side till brown. These shrimp may be frozen after they have been cooked, with or without the dressing, for about one month. Partially defrost before broiling.

LOBSTER THERMIDOR
SERVES 4

two 1½-lb. lobsters, boiled
¼ cup oil
¾ cup sliced mushrooms
½ t. dry mustard
1 T. minced parsley
dash paprika
½ cup sherry wine
2 T. grated Parmesan cheese
1½ cups cream sauce

Cream Sauce:

3 T. oil
3 T. flour
1½ cups milk
½ t. salt (preferably vegetable)

Cook lobsters in a large kettle of boiling water adding 2 T. salt for each quart of water. Bring to a boil and simmer 20 minutes. If you are using frozen lobster tails, cook as package directs.

Make cream sauce while lobster is cooking. Heat oil, stir in flour. When well blended, gradually add milk. Add salt. Cook till thickened. Set aside.

Remove lobster from water when done. Cut lobsters lengthwise into halves and remove meat. Break it into small chunks. Saute mushrooms for 5 minutes in oil. Add the mustard, parsley, paprika, and sherry to 1 cup of the cream sauce. Add lobster meat and mushrooms to cream sauce. Fill lobster shells or oiled ramekins with creamed lobster. Cover with remaining cream sauce, sprinkle with cheese, and bake at 450°F. for 10 minutes, till top is slightly browned.

SOUPS

CREAM OF CHESTNUT SOUP
SERVES 4

1 lb. chestnuts (in shells)
1 medium onion, diced
2 T. oil
one medium carrot
2 cups chicken stock (not bouillon cubes)
¾ cup light cream or top milk
1 T. raw sugar

Prepare the chestnuts by slitting crosswise. Cover with boiling water and boil 15 minutes. Remove one at a time, put under cold water, and skin. Saute the diced onion in the oil till lightly browned (about 3 to 5 minutes). Add the onion to the chestnuts. Peel the carrot and cut into ½-inch slices. Add to the chestnuts. Add the chicken stock. Bring to a boil, turn heat down, and simmer till chestnuts are soft, about 15 minutes. Pour liquid through a colander and save it. Puree or blend the chestnuts. Return to the broth and heat. Add light cream or top milk and the sugar. Heat, but don't boil, and serve.

CREAM OF CARROT SOUP
SERVES 4 TO 6

2 cups carrots, cut into 1-inch pieces
1½ cups chicken stock
½ t. salt (preferably vegetable)
2 cups light cream or top milk

Cook the carrot pieces in boiling water, covered, till tender. Drain. Save the cooking water to make up the chicken stock. Blend the carrots, or puree them if you lack a blender. Add the chicken stock and salt and blend. Add the light cream or top milk and blend. Heat to simmering and serve.

Variations: 2 cups other vegetables, such as cauliflower, corn, celery, spinach, asparagus, or mushrooms, may be substituted for the carrots. The mushrooms would have to be sauteed in 3 T. oil rather than being boiled.

MINESTRONE
(Italian Vegetable Soup)
MAKES 2 QTS., SERVES 4 TO 6 AS MAIN COURSE

¼ cup oil, preferably olive oil
¼ to ½ lb. ground beef or ground round steak
1 stalk celery
2 medium carrots
1 small onion
½ small green or red cabbage
1 cup canned or stewed tomatoes
1 cup dry kidney beans, soaked overnight
in water to cover (or substitute 2 cups canned
kidney beans)
1 clove garlic, finely minced
½ cup brown rice, uncooked
1 qt. beef stock (cubes may be used)
1 t. salt (preferably vegetable salt)
¼ t. pepper (preferably freshly ground)
2 T. grated Parmesan cheese

Place oil in a pressure cooker without rack, add the ground beef and cook till brown. Chop the celery and carrots. Dice the onion. Slice the cabbage fine. Mince the onion. Add the vegetables, kidney beans with the water they were soaking in, rice, beef stock, salt, pepper, and garlic. Put cover on pressure cooker (never have a pressure cooker more than ⅔ full) and turn on high heat. Exhaust the cooker of air for about 5 minutes, place on petcock and bring to 15 lbs. pressure. Turn down heat, or move to a cooler burner, and allow to cook for 15 minutes at 15 lbs. pressure. Remove from burner and allow pressure to return to normal. Remove cover carefully, sprinkle with cheese and serve. This will make a meal with Italian or French bread and a salad.

Note—If you don't have a pressure cooker, simmer this soup for 1½ hours or till beans and rice are tender.

PUREE MONGOLE
SERVES 6

1 cup dried split peas
1 medium onion, diced
2 T. oil
2 cups tomato juice
5 cups water
1 t. pepper (preferably freshly ground)

Cover peas with the water and soak overnight. Heat oil in a 3-qt. saucepan and saute the onion till golden (about 5 minutes). Add the peas with the water, tomato juice, salt, and pepper. Bring to a boil, turn down the heat and simmer covered 45 minutes. Sieve through a food mill, or blend in a blender.

Note—Soaking of peas may be omitted—cook 15 minutes extra.

SPINACH SOUP
SERVES 6

2 lbs. fresh spinach, or 2 10-oz. pkgs. frozen
spinach (chopped)
1 medium onion, minced
3 T. oil
3 T. flour
6 cups chicken stock (not bouillon cubes)
pinch rosemary
¼ t. pepper (preferably freshly ground)

Clean spinach well in several waters. Remove all
stems and discolored portions. Cook till just tender
(about 5 to 10 minutes) in a covered saucepan with
just the water that clings to the leaves. Drain and
chop very fine. Cook frozen spinach if you are substituting that. In a 3-qt. saucepan saute the minced
onion in the oil till transparent but not brown. Blend
in the flour and half of the chicken stock. Cool till
blended, add remaining stock, pepper, and rosemary.
Bring to a boil. Add the spinach, heat throughly, and
serve.

LENTIL SOUP
SERVES 8

2 qts. beef stock, preferably made from beef
stock base
1½ cups lentils
1 cracked ham bone (optional)
2 stalks celery
2 carrots
1 t. salt (preferably vegetable salt)
½ t. monosodium glutamate
¼ t. pepper
3 sprigs parsley or 2 T. dried parsley
2 T. oil
2 medium onions, thinly sliced
6 frankfurters (optional)

Make up beef stock and bring to a boil. Add the
lentils, ham bone, diced celery, sliced and peeled
carrots, salt, monosodium glutamate, pepper, and
parsley. Bring to a boil, reduce heat, and simmer till
lentils are tender, about 1 to 1½ hours. Remove ham
bone from soup. Sieve soup or blend in a blender.
Saute the 2 thinly sliced onions in the oil with the
frankfurters cut into ½-inch slices till onions are transparent and frankfurters are lightly browned. Add to
soup and simmer 10 minutes.

SAUCES

MUSTARD SAUCE
MAKES 1 CUP
(VERY GOOD OVER CAULIFLOWER OR WITH
LEFTOVER HAM)

1 T. oil
2 T. flour, preferably unbleached white
1 cup milk
3 T. mayonnaise
1½ T. prepared yellow mustard
1 T. lemon juice
¼ t. salt (preferably vegetable salt)
dash pepper (preferably freshly ground)

Place oil in the top of a double boiler over boiling water. Stir in the flour and add milk gradually till thickened. Add mayonnaise, mustard, lemon juice, salt, and pepper. Heat till warm. Will keep refrigerated several days. Always reheat over hot water.

This may be served over a whole cooked cauliflower or over small pieces of cooked cauliflower.

CREAM SAUCE

2 T. oil
2 T. flour, preferably unbleached white
1 cup milk
¼ t. salt (preferably vegetable salt)
dash pepper (preferably freshly ground)

Place oil in a small saucepan over medium heat and stir in flour. Add milk gradually till thickened. Add salt and pepper.

Variation: Cheese Sauce: Add ½ cup grated mild or sharp cheese and heat over low heat till cheese is melted.

Note—For a thin sauce, use 1 T. oil and 1 T. flour. For a thick sauce use 4 T. oil and 4 T. flour.

GRAVY
MAKES 2 ½ CUPS

Beef Gravy:

2 T. oil and 2 T. pan drippings, or 4 T. oil
1¾ cups beef stock, preferably made from beef stock base
3 T. arrowroot dissolved in ½ cup cold water
1 t. Kitchen Bouquet seasoning
salt and pepper to taste

Chicken or Turkey Gravy:

2 T. oil and 2 T. pan drippings, or 4 T. oil
3 T. arrowroot dissolved in ½ cup cold w ater
1¾ cups chicken stock, preferably made from chicken stock base
salt and pepper to taste
¼ t. poultry seasoning, if desired

Heat oil and drippings with stock till hot. Dissolve arrowroot in cold water. Gradually stir it into the hot oil and stock mixture, stirring constantly. Cook over moderate heat 1 to 2 minutes till thickened and somewhat clear. Add seasonings. Taste for salt.

Variation: Giblet gravy: Add ½ cup finely chopped

chicken or turkey giblets, which have been cooked. You may use the giblet broth to make up the chicken stock, but if the giblet broth is very salty, don't make the chicken stock as strong as usual.

SECRET BARBECUE SAUCE
MAKES 2 CUPS

1 medium chopped onion
1 clove garlic, minced
½ cup raisins
½ cup (1 6-oz. can) tomato paste
2 T. cider vinegar
1 t. dry mustard
⅔ cup oil
½ t. basil
½ t. monosodium glutamate
⅛ t. each rosemary, thyme, and marjoram
¼ cup brown sugar, packed
1 t. salt, preferably vegetable
1 T. lemon juice
¼ t. black pepper
2 T. Worcestershire sauce
½ cup red wine, Burgundy type (optional)

Mix all ingredients together and blend in a blender about 15 seconds. Otherwise, chop onion, garlic, and raisins very fine and add to other ingredients. Cook in the top of a double boiler, uncovered, for 1 hour, stirring often. Serve with chicken, beef, or spareribs. Marinate meat ½ to 1 hour before broiling or grilling and baste frequently.

VEGETABLES

Vegetables deserve special cooking effort since they are rich in vitamins and minerals (if properly prepared), are frequently low in calories, and often are good food buys. With all these virtues, they are still often scorned by many people, usually because they are not properly prepared.

For the best vegetables, grow your own organically if you can.

GREEN BEANS ALMONDINE
SERVES 4

1 lb. fresh green beans (frozen may be substituted)
½ cup blanched, slivered almonds
¼ cup butter or margarine

Wash beans and snip off the ends. Cook in a covered saucepan with a moderate amount of water till tender. This will depend on the size and freshness of the beans (up to 30 to 40 minutes). Small fresh beans may cook in 15 minutes. Meanwhile, prepare the almonds. Boil the almonds in water to cover for a few minutes in order to get the brown skin off. Drain, slip off skins, sliver, and cook in butter over medium heat till lightly browned, stirring with a fork constantly. When beans are done, drain them, saving the cooking water for soup. Reheat the almonds till sizzling and pour them hot over the beans. Season beans with a little salt if desired.

LOUISIANA GREEN BEANS
SERVES 6

1 lb. fresh cooked green beans
6 slices bacon
1 small onion, minced
one green pepper, minced
2 cups canned or stewed tomatoes
1½ t. Worcestershire sauce
1 T. brown sugar
1 t. salt (preferably vegetable)

Cook green beans till tender. Drain. Fry bacon till crisp and drain on paper towel. Pour off drippings, except 2 T. Mince onion and green pepper and saute in the remaining bacon fat in skillet for about 2 minutes, till onion is transparent, but not browned. Add remaining ingredients with the beans, cover, and simmer 15 minutes. Taste for seasoning.

BEETS IN POMEGRANATE SAUCE
SERVES 4

4 medium beets
½ cup pomegranate juice (from one medium pomegranate)
2 t. arrowroot
1 T. honey
¼ t. salt (preferably vegetable salt)

Scrub beets. Save the tops for another meal if

they are fresh enough. The tops contain more vitamins and minerals than the roots and may be cooked just like spinach. Leave 1 inch of the root on to prevent bleeding of the beets. Cook in boiling water till tender (up to 30 to 40 minutes depending on size of beets). I prefer to cook my beets in a pressure cooker at 15 lbs. pressure for 15 to 20 minutes. While beets are cooking, make the pomegranate juice by peeling the pomegranate and pressing the seeds through a sieve to make ½ cup juice. Be careful not to mix any of the white part underneath the skin with the seeds, as this is very bitter. In a small saucepan stir the juice gradually into the arrowroot. Add the honey and cook over medium heat till thickened. Slip the skin off the cooked beets, slice, and add to the sauce. Heat and serve, seasoning with the salt if desired.

BEETS IN ORANGE SAUCE
SERVES 4

¼ cup oil
2 T. flour, preferably unbleached white
2 T. light brown sugar
1 cup orange juice
½ salt (preferably vegetable)
1 T. lemon juice
1 T. grated orange rind
2 cups sliced cooked beets (canned beets may be substituted)

Place oil in a medium saucepan and heat. Stir in the flour and sugar. Gradually add the orange juice and cook till thickened. Stir in the salt and lemon juice. Add the orange rind. Stir in the beets, heat, and serve.

TANGY BROCCOLI
SERVES 4 TO 6

1 bunch broccoli
¼ cup butter or margarine
2 T. lemon juice
salt and pepper

Wash broccoli. Peel off tough outside skin. Cut lengthwise into pieces about ½ to 1 inch in diameter; keep pieces fairly even in size so they will all cook in the same amount of time. Steam for 10 to 15 minutes in an upright position (tying if necessary) till tender but not mushy. Cooking upright prevents the tops from overcooking. I use a baby bottle sterilizer, placing the broccoli stems in the bottle holes on the inserted rack. This works for asparagus as well. Melt butter and stir in lemon juice. When broccoli is tender, lift out carefully, with tongs if necessary, place on serving dish, pour lemon butter over broccoli, season with salt and pepper, and serve.

Note—if you don't have a bottle sterilizer, try using a coffee pot. You may need to tie the broccoli in a bunch to give it support as it may collapse into the water when it softens.

BRUSSELS SPROUTS
IN MUSHROOM SAUCE
SERVES 4

1 pt. Brussels sprouts, fresh or frozen
1 can cream of mushroom soup
½ cup milk
salt and pepper

Wash fresh Brussels sprouts, removing any discolored outer leaves. Cook in boiling water till tender (about 10 to 15 minutes). Drain. Heat the soup with the milk, add the Brussels sprouts, and heat. Season with salt and pepper.

TROPICAL CARROTS
SERVES 4

6 medium carrots, cut into 1-inch pieces and cooked
1 T. arrowroot
1 T. honey
½ cup canned crushed pineapple (preferably packed in its own juice without sugar), drained
¼ t. salt
1 T. butter, margarine, or oil

Peel and slice carrots into 1-inch pieces. Place in a saucepan with water to barely cover. Bring to a boil, cover, reduce heat, and simmer till tender (about 7 to 10 minutes). Drain. Place arrowroot in a medium saucepan and gradually stir in the pineapple juice. Add the honey. Cook over medium heat, stirring constantly till thickened. Stir in the drained pineapple, salt, and butter or oil. Heat slightly, add the carrots, heat, and serve.

MINT GLAZED CARROTS WITH PEAS
SERVES 4

3 medium carrots
2 cups cooked peas, fresh or frozen
⅛ cup margarine or butter
¼ cup honey
½ to 1 t. mint extract (depending on how minty you like it)
salt and pepper

Peel carrots and cut into lengthwise slices ¼ inch thick. Cut into 2-inch strips. Cook in boiling water to barely cover till tender about (5 minutes) and drain. Cook peas till tender in boiling water to barely cover (about 5 minutes for frozen peas or 10 to 12 minutes for fresh peas). Drain. In a medium saucepan melt butter or margarine, add honey, mint extract, and carrots. Cook uncovered slowly till carrots are well glazed, stirring occasionally (about 5 to 10 minutes). Add peas. Season with salt and pepper, if desired, and heat and serve.

CAULIFLOWER WALDINE
SERVES 6

one medium head cauliflower
¼ cup butter or margarine
¼ cup chopped walnuts
few sprigs parsley, chopped
1 t. salt (preferably vegetable)

Break cauliflower into flowerlets and cook in boiling water till barely tender, about 5 to 10 minutes. Never overcook cauliflower or it will lose its flavor. Drain. Melt butter, stir in nuts and chopped parsley with the salt and pepper, if desired, pour over cauliflower, and serve.

CAULIFLOWER WITH CARROT ROSES
SERVES 6

1 medium cauliflower
2 medium carrots
¼ cup butter or margarine
2 T. honey
1 T. lemon juice
parsley

Wash cauliflower and remove outer leaves and part of center stem, so that the cauliflower will sit flat on a dish. Place whole in a proper-sized pan, top side down in pan, cover with boiling water and simmer till tender but still slightly crisp (about 15 to 20 minutes). Drain carefully, placing on serving platter. While cauliflower is cooking, prepare carrot roses. Peel carrots and cut into 1-inch lengths. Notch top of carrot pieces to resemble a flower. Make 7 to 8 carrot roses. Trim lower edge to a thick point. Simmer in water till tender (about 3 to 5 minutes). Drain. Melt butter in a small saucepan, add honey and drained carrot roses and glaze for about 5 minutes. When cauliflower is ready, slash it in 7 or 8 places on crown of cauliflower and place the carrot roses into these slashes. Add the lemon juice to the remaining butter-honey mixture, heat, and pour it all over the cauliflower. Outline the cauliflower with parsley and you have your bouquet of orange roses.

CREAMED FRESH MUSHROOMS
SERVES 4

15 large fresh mushrooms (about ¾ lb.) frozen
mushrooms may be substituted
3 T. butter or margarine
5 T. butter or margarine
5 T. flour, preferably unbleached white flour
¾ cup double strength beef stock
¼ t. salt (preferably vegetable salt)
dash pepper (preferably freshly ground)
¾ cup milk
½ t. Worcestershire sauce

Wipe the mushrooms with a damp cloth. Don't
peel unless they are discolored. Slice lengthwise
into ¼-inch slices, slicing through stem and top so
they remain in one piece. Saute the mushrooms in
the 3 T. butter for 5 minutes, stirring frequently.
Make sauce: Melt butter, stir in flour. Add the beef
stock gradually. Add milk gradually and cook, stirring constantly, till thickened. Add salt, pepper, and
Worcestershire sauce. Add mushrooms, heat, and
serve. This is good with broiled steak.

OVEN BROWNED POTATOES
SERVES 6

6 medium potatoes
½ t. salt
3 T. melted butter or oil

Peel potatoes, cut into ½-inch cubes, cover with
boiling water, add salt, and simmer 5 minutes. Drain.
Spread potatoes in a shallow baking pan, drizzle
melted butter or oil over all and bake at 400°F. for
about 30 to 40 minutes till nicely browned and
crusty. Stir occasionally with a fork to prevent
burning.

PAPRIKA POTATOES
SERVES 6

2 lbs. uniform-sized small new potatoes
3 T. butter, margarine, or oil
1 T. paprika
½ t. salt (preferably vegetable salt)

Wash potatoes, but don't peel. Cook in boiling water to cover till just done (barely tender). This will depend on the size of the potatoes, but will probably take 10 to 15 minutes. Drain, slip off the skins, and chill in refrigerator, covered, several hours or overnight. At serving time, melt butter in skillet, add potatoes, coat them well, using a wooden spoon to roll them in the butter, and sprinkle evenly with the paprika and salt. Make sure potatoes are heated through, and serve.

RICE ALMONDINE
SERVES 4

2 cups hot cooked brown rice
½ cup slivered blanched almonds
¼ cup butter or margarine
⅜ cup ripe olives, slivered or chopped
½ t. salt (preferably vegetable salt)
¼ t. pepper (preferably freshly ground)

Cook rice. You will need about ⅔ cup uncooked rice. Cook the rice for about 40 minutes, till tender, in 2 cups boiling water. To prevent burning, I like to use a double boiler to cook rice. Cover the rice while cooking. Drain when done. To blanch almonds, simmer them in boiling water for 5 minutes. Drain, slip off skins, and sliver. Melt butter, add almonds, and saute the almonds over medium heat till slightly browned, stirring constantly. Sliver olives. If you use chopped olives, drain them. When rice is done, stir in the almonds, olives, salt and pepper and serve.

SAUTEED ACORN SQUASH
SERVES 4

one 2-lb. acorn squash
3 T. butter
½ t. salt (preferably vegetable salt)
3 T. brown sugar
¼ t. ground nutmeg (preferably freshly ground)

Cut squash in half and scoop out seed and fiber in center. Cut squash lengthwise along the lines of the outside grooves. Peel off the green skin with a vegetable peeler, if desired. Cut squash into ¼-inch slices. Cut these slices into 2-inch lengths. Melt butter in a skillet, add squash, sprinkle with salt, cover, and cook over medium heat 5 minutes. Use a pancake turner to turn squash over. Add the sugar and nutmeg, cover tightly, and cook 5 minutes, or till tender, translucent, and slightly browned.

APRICOT CANDIED SWEET POTATOES
SERVES 6 TO 8

2 lbs. peeled, cooked sweet potatoes
1 cup cooked, drained dried apricots (preferably unsulphured)
¼ t. salt
¼ cup melted butter, margarine, or oil
1 cup brown sugar, packed
¼ cup liquid from apricots
1 t. grated orange rind.
¼ cup grated coconut

Cook the peeled sweet potatoes in boiling water till just tender. Drain and cut into 1-inch thick crosswise slices. Grease a 10 x 6 x 2-inch baking dish. Arrange half of the sweet potato slices in bottom of baking dish. Arrange half of the apricots over the sweet potatoes. Melt butter, add brown sugar, salt, apricot liquid, and orange rind. Bring to a boil and simmer 5 minutes. Remove from heat and pour half of this mixture over the sweet potatoes in the baking dish. Arrange remaining potatoes over this sugar layer; arrange remaining apricots on the potatoes and pour remaining syrup over all. Bake at 375°F. for 30 minutes. Sprinkle ¼ cup of coconut over top, return to oven and bake another 15 minutes to toast coconut. Serve. This will freeze if you have leftovers.

CURRIED TOMATOES
SERVES 6

6 medium tomatoes
1 cup tomato sauce
½ t. curry powder
1 T. honey
¼ t. salt (preferably vegetable salt)
⅛ t. pepper (preferably freshly ground)
dash ground nutmeg
1 T. butter or margarine
2 T. grated Parmesan cheese
½ t. dried oregano

Place tomatoes in a medium saucepan, cover with boiling water, and let stand 5 minutes. Drain, peel, and remove cores. Place tomatoes in an oiled deep baking dish or casserole. In a small saucepan combine the tomato sauce, curry powder, honey, salt and pepper, and nutmeg. Bring to a boil and simmer 5 minutes. Stir in 1 T. butter. Sprinkle the tomatoes with the cheese and oregano. Cover with sauce and bake at 400°F. for 20 minutes.

ORIENTAL SPINACH
SERVES 4

1 lb. fresh spinach
2 T. oil
¼ t. garlic powder
1 t. salt (preferably vegetable salt)
¼ t. pepper
½ t. raw sugar
¼ t. monosodium glutamate

Wash spinach well, remove stems and any discolored portions. Heat oil in a large saucepan, add spinach, and stir till spinach leaves are well coated with oil. Add remaining ingredients, stir in well, cover, and cook 3 to 4 minutes over moderate heat till spinach is wilted and tender.

SNOW PEAS WITH WATER CHESTNUTS
SERVES 4

2 cups snow peas, or sugar peas (These are tiny Chinese peas which are eaten in the pod. Just remove the stem with the string that runs down the center of the pod. Two cups fresh or frozen regular peas may be substituted for the snow peas, since snow peas are almost unobtainable in most stores. If you want to taste them, you will probably have to grow them yourself.)

2 T. oil
½ cup sliced water chestnuts (canned)
1 t. monosodium glutamate
1 cup chicken stock
2 t. arrowroot mixed with 2 T. cold water

Heat 2 T. oil in medium-sized saucepan and add snow peas. Stir peas till well coated with oil. Add sliced water chestnuts, monosodium glutamate, and chicken stock. Cover and simmer 3 to 5 minutes. Snow peas should not be cooked until they are soft; they should be slightly crisp. Mix arrowroot with cold water, add to peas, and cook till thick and glazy.

TURNIPS IN CHICKEN STOCK
SERVES 4

1½ lbs. white turnips
1 cup chicken stock
1 T. lemon juice
1 T. butter or margarine

Peel turnips and cut into ½-inch slices. Mix together the chicken stock, lemon juice, and butter and bring to a boil. Add turnip slices, cover, and simmer till tender (about 15 to 20 minutes). Drain and serve.

Note—Other vegetables, such as Brussels sprouts, are good cooked in chicken stock.

MASHED YELLOW TURNIPS (RUTABAGA)
SERVES 4 TO 6

1 medium rutabaga
2 medium potatoes
4 carrots
2 T. butter or margarine
½ t. salt (preferably vegetable salt)
¼ t. pepper (preferably freshly ground)

Peel rutabaga and cut into ½-inch slices. Peel and cut potatoes into quarters. Peel carrots and cut into 1-inch chunks. Cook all these vegetables together in boiling water till tender, 20 to 25 minutes. I cook them in a pressure cooker for 10 minutes at 15 lbs. pressure. Drain and put through a potato ricer. Add about 2 T. of the liquid in which vegetables were cooked to give the proper consistency to the mashed vegetables. Add butter, salt and pepper, and serve.

CHINESE FRIED RICE WITH BACON, TOMATO, AND LETTUCE
SERVES 4

8 slices diced bacon
6 leaves sliced lettuce
2 cups sliced onions
2 cups cooked and cooled brown rice
¼ cup soy sauce
½ t. monosodium glutamate
¼ t. pepper (preferably freshly ground)
½ t. salt
2 diced fresh tomatoes (or substitute canned)
water if necessary.

Fry bacon till done. Pour off excess fat. Add sliced lettuce and onions and fry 1 minute, stirring constantly. Add rice, soy sauce, monosodium glutamate, pepper, and salt. Cook and stir 2 minutes, adding a little water if necessary to keep from burning. Add diced tomato and stir to heat. Serve.

BEVERAGES

∞∞∞∞∞∞∞∞∞∞∞

CAROB SYRUP
MAKES 1½ CUPS
(FOR USE AS FLAVORING FOR MILK OR AS A
DESSERT SAUCE ON ICE CREAM)

1 cup carob powder
1¼ cups water
½ cup honey
1 t. vanilla extract

Stir water into the carob powder, adding it slowly and stirring well. Add honey. Bring to a boil. Boil 2 minutes, stirring constantly. Cool. Add vanilla. Refrigerate. Use 1 to 2 T. of the syrup to flavor 8 oz. of milk.

Variation: Carob Mint Syrup: Substitute ¼ t. mint extract for the vanilla.

STRAWBERRY PUNCH
SERVES 4 TO 6

2 cups water
½ cup honey
1 cup fresh or frozen strawberries and 1 cup water
juice of 1 orange
juice of 3 lemons
1 cup pineapple juice

Bring the 2 cups of water mixed with the ½ cup of honey to a boil. Simmer 1 minute, till honey is dissolved. Cool. Bring the 1 cup of strawberries combined with 1 cup of water to a boil. Simmer 5 minutes. Strain through cheesecloth to make strawberry juice. Cool. Combine the honey syrup, strawberry juice, and other juices. Let stand for a couple of hours in the refrigerator to allow flavors to blend. Serve cold.

LIME APRICOT COOLER
SERVES 4

1 cup mint syrup
1 qt. apricot nectar
½ cup lime juice
ice

Mix the mint syrup, apricot nectar, and lime juice together. Pour over ice in tall glasses. Garnish with a mint sprig if desired.

PEPPERMINT TEA
SERVES 4

1 qt. water
½ cup fresh or frozen mint leaves

Bring water to a boil. Add mint leaves. Simmer 2 minutes. Strain into cups. Serve with honey if desired.

Note: Dried mint leaves may be substituted for the fresh. Use half as much mint. If you prefer a weaker tea, steep the tea for 2 minutes instead of simmering it.

STRAWBERRY MILKSHAKE
SERVES 2

1½ cups milk
½ cup powdered skim milk
1 cup fresh or frozen unsweetened strawberries
¼ cup honey

Place all ingredients in a blender and blend till frothy, about 30 seconds. Serve immediately.

Variation: Banana. Use 2 mashed bananas in place of the strawberries and omit honey.

Note: If you don't have a blender, beat together in a bowl with an electric mixer, but mash the fruit first.

PINEAPPLE ORANGE FRAPPE
SERVES 4

1 envelope unflavored gelatin
¼ cup cold water
2 T. lemon juice
1 cup crushed canned pineapple with juice (preferably packed in its own juice with no sugar added)
one 12-oz. can frozen orange juice concentrate
2 cups crushed ice

Soften gelatin in cold water for 5 minutes. Dissolve over hot water. Pour lemon juice and pineapple into a blender. Blend a few seconds. Add dissolved gelatin, orange juice concentrate, and crushed ice and blend until of a sherbet-like consistency. Add the ice gradually. Turn into chilled glasses and serve immediately. Garnish with orange slices if desired.

SNOWBALLS
(FOR THE CHILDREN)

Allow about 6 ice cubes for each child. Crush the ice, then put it into the blender a little at a time and blend till like "snow." Remove the "snow" as you go along if you are making any quantity of snowballs, so that you can get all the ice crushed equally fine. Spoon the "snow" into individual paper cups and let the children pour whatever flavor fruit juice they like over their snowballs. If they prefer mint flavor, use 2 T. of the following Mint Syrup for each snowball.

MINT SYRUP
MAKES 2 CUPS

1 cup water
1 cup raw sugar or honey
⅔ cup fresh or frozen mint leaves, chopped

Bring water and sugar or honey to a boil. Add mint leaves. Simmer 5 minutes. Strain. Refrigerate.